LACANIAN TREATMENT

LACANIAN TREATMENT
Psychoanalysis for Clinicians

Yehuda Israely

Routledge
Taylor & Francis Group

LONDON AND NEW YORK

The original book was published in Hebrew by Resling Publishers in Israel (2014).
Edited by Idan Oren.
Translated to English by Mirjam Hadar.

First published in English 2018
by Routledge
2 Park Square, Milton Park, Abingdon, Oxon OX14 4RN

and by Routledge
711 Third Avenue, New York, NY 10017

Routledge is an imprint of the Taylor & Francis Group, an informa business

British Library Cataloguing-in-Publication Data
A catalogue record for this book is available from the British Library

Library of Congress Cataloging-in-Publication Data
A catalog record has been requested for this book

ISBN: 978-1-78220-618-7 (pbk)

Typeset in Palatino LT Std
by Medlar Publishing Solutions Pvt Ltd, India

CONTENTS

ACKNOWLEDGEMENTS   vii

PREFACE   ix

INTRODUCTION   xiii

CHAPTER ONE
Ethical foundations   1

CHAPTER TWO
The clinic as a symbolic space   29

CHAPTER THREE
Transference   49

CHAPTER FOUR
Symptom   57

CHAPTER FIVE
Trauma, anguish, and depression   67

v

CHAPTER SIX
Clinical structures as subject positions   75

CHAPTER SEVEN
The end of treatment   87

NOTES   93

REFERENCES   95

INDEX   99

ACKNOWLEDGEMENTS

Even if it is the psychoanalyst's role to be an object in the clinic, it is, nevertheless, a subject who assumes this role. And so, these words of gratitude for support received in the course of writing this book, are part and parcel of my gratitude for being a subject, a psychoanalyst, and, finally an author. First and foremost, therefore, I thank mother Shoshana, of blessed memory, and my father Eitan, who raised me so very lovingly. Thanks to my extended family, my father's wife Valey, my brothers and sister, their partners and children—the very fabric in which I belong. Thanks to the teachers, trainers, therapists, and psychoanalysts who accompanied me on my personal and professional journey and acquainted me with the secrets of the unconscious: Andre Patsalides, Amir Schneider, Collette Soler, Luis Izcovich, and Sarah Ivanir. I would like to thank my friends at the Tel Aviv Forum of the Lacanian Field, my comrades in the analyst's desire, for their partnership in the journey. Thanks to my patients and students, throughout the years: all of them enlightened me; and special thanks to those who agreed for me to use anonymous illustrations from their lives for this book. Special thanks to my friend Idan Oren who edited this book with dedication, meticulously, and with great talent; and thanks to Mirjam Hadar for her apt and eloquent translation. My gratitude, too, to my children and their partners, Dor, Anat, Ella, and Nir, as well as to Naama and Lavi, my grandchildren, for their generous support, attention, and love. More than anyone, I thank my wife Osnat, love of my life, who leaves the marks of goodness on every part of my life: this book is no exception.

PREFACE

Jacques Marie Emile Lacan was born in France in 1901, one year after the publication of Freud's monumental *The Interpretation of Dreams*, which for many signals the inception of psychoanalysis. Lacan died in 1981, after twenty-eight years of teaching psychoanalysis. He dedicated most of his time to study, reading, treating patients, and encouraging his students to read. Students who stayed with him until his end report that they sighed with relief once they no longer had to cope with the amount of reading he imposed on them.

A psychiatrist by training, Lacan was constantly reading—in all fields of science and the humanities. The knowledge thus gained, he brought to bear in his expansive project, formulating a complex and extremely original theory and practice. This work was grounded in Freud's psychoanalysis and on a strong ethical position. Like Freud before him, Lacan challenged prevalent views and values—some of which survive to this day. He never held back his criticism of the work of many theoreticians, mainly those who followed in Freud's footsteps. This, together with his bold innovations, like for instance cutting the analytic hour, aroused antagonism among the leading figures in the International Psychoanalytic Association (IPA) and his status as didactic psychoanalyst was withdrawn. Considering himself excommunicated, just like

Spinoza, his hero, he established his own psychoanalytic organisation in 1964—L'Ecole Freudienne de Paris (EFP). When, in 1980, he felt that the EFP was falling into a dogmatism reminiscent of the IPA, he dissolved the organisation. Lacan believed that Freud had failed to prevent the politicisation of the IPA, and had at times compromised his own position in order to avoid antagonism. Instead of the EFP, Lacan established L'Ecole de la Cause Freudienne. Over a thousand applications for membership arrived in its first week alone.

Lacan applied his insights about human nature and the dangers of dogmatism in the way he gave shape to organisational culture. He evolved, for instance, mechanisms that were aimed to prevent the development of imaginary authorities (on the Imaginary, see below). Thus the "pass" constitutes an encounter between one who recently concluded her or his analysis, and other psychoanalysts: here the former reports on her or his experience in order to contribute to the psychoanalytic body of knowledge. Thus the "cartel" is a study group that meets for a set period of time—with the aim to avoid the emergence of foci of power—whether social or political—which take their toll on the development of knowledge.

Not unlike the topological models he used to illustrate his ideas, Lacan himself had a paradoxical personality. Even though he was extremely influential, he wrote very little. Most of his published work was copied from the seminars he conducted. And while he did not consider himself a philosopher his work played a pivotal role in post-structuralist philosophy and was taught in departments of philosophy, literature, and art worldwide. In fact, he criticised philosophers, among other things, for their way of looking at statements without taking into account that they were made by subjects. So, for instance he censured the philosopher Jacques Derrida, himself a crucial representative of post-modernism, arguing that the latter allowed himself to deconstruct everything only because he wasn't responsible for treating people's problems. For Lacan, philosophy, theory, and topology were of no value outside the context of their effect on human beings. Though there are some exceptions, like Nietzsche or Wittgenstein, who, like Lacan mentioned the role of philosophy in the actual lives people live—they too never treated real people: Lacan's point of departure, by contrast, was the clinic.

Lacan remained faithful to Freud's original discoveries regarding the central role of the unconscious and of sexuality in the life of the mind

(Lacan, 1988 [1953], pp. 15 & 21). He describes the beginnings of psychoanalysis as the point in human history at which the unconscious was uncovered. The contemporary opposition from both scientists and intellectuals was so powerful, that even Josef Breuer, Freud's colleague and collaborator at the time he discovered the unconscious, publicly distanced himself. After Freud's death, the discovery of the unconscious—with its huge implication for our concept of the human—evaporated like the memory of a dream once we awake. In his attempt to undermine the closure of the unconscious Lacan took the position of a psychoanalyst, too. A clear illustration of the fading of Freud's discovery, he believed, was found in what is known as "ego psychology", whose main therapeutic objective is the ego's adaptation to the demands of normativity.

Opposition to Freud's ideas in his lifetime, according to Lacan, continued after his death, among his followers. Such notions as infantile sexuality continued to arouse aversion among audiences, and many of his students too repressed them. Thus, for instance, only few theoreticians took on the ideas of the death drive and the castration complex. Nowadays, too, university departments of psychology hardly teach either Freud or Lacan. The critique of the Neo-Freudian interpretations of some of Freud's followers that forms the core of Lacan's theory still threatens many schools of psychoanalysis and clinical psychology.

INTRODUCTION

Psychoanalytic knowledge, traditionally, is considered the psychoanalyst's domain in his individual work with patients. But this knowledge is also valuable to people working and thinking outside that immediate context.[1]

This book, offering a framework for thought and action drawing on the theory of Jacques Lacan, may serve all those treating the psyche (whether they are psychotherapists, couple therapists, art therapists, or youth workers in a psychiatric unit). The Lacanian perspective restores attention to certain Freudian insights neglected by other schools of thought, while also proposing adjustments and innovations to some Freudian ideas. This is why in this book, when I use the term "analysis" or "analyst", it could very well be a therapist in psychotherapy, who is not necessarily a trained analyst, who could make use of this knowledge. It is up to the practitioners who read the book to adapt the content to their needs, to their professional self-description, or in Lacan's words: to subjectify it.

The notion of *subjectivisation*—the construction of reality in terms of the subject's particular relation to the world—central to Lacan's thinking, also holds for any subject's position *vis-a-vis* a theory. It follows that this book's Lacanian and Freudian positions are the author's interpretation of Lacan's and Freud's writings. Thus, for instance a central axis of the present reading is its understanding of the symptom as an expression of repressed desire, in the spirit of Freud, but with the addition of the Lacanian understanding that the symptom not only expresses desire but also produces it.

Lacanian treatment is first and foremost a craft of working with words. It was Freud who said that the very aim of psychoanalysis is to use words in solving problems caused by words. These are the words forming the cultural environment that have shaped the patient. As they interconnect they determine meanings and forms of pleasure that eventually come to structure his identity. Lacanian thought perceives the patient's identity as a symbolic texture of words. The more fully the analyst subscribes to the notion that reality is a function of meanings and of words—that is, that reality is symbolical rather than actual or natural, as positivist philosophy would have it, or as the patient will tend to believe at the early stages of treatment—the more will words work in the service of the treatment as the patient makes changes to his life.

In the Lacanian perspective, a central component of analysts' training is the analysis they themselves have undergone. Interpretations heard when they were analysands are assumed to have changed the meanings of words engraved on their psyche, thus changing the modes of desire and pleasure associated with these words. Such exposure to the power of words spoken in early childhood and to the power of words spoken as part of interpretations in treatment is a precondition for the work with words they are to do as analysts.

The treatment's objectives and outcomes—reflected in the subject's ability to take an analytic position—are situated in the ethical domain. Ethics addresses questions concerning the nature of the proper action and values to be pursued. A precondition to dealing with such issues is one's formulation of the nature of reality. This is why the first chapter of this book discusses Lacanian psychoanalysis' fundamental assumptions regarding reality, and the status of language in this reality, as well as the ethical values entailed by these philosophical assumptions. Lacan's most basic assumption regarding reality is that reality is an assumption. The riddle which the psychoanalyst tries to solve is how the patient constructs his reality by way of an assumption that is both outcome of his symptom and validated by it. More simply put: What is the story which a person inhabits so as to maintain his desire and how does the symptom validate this story as a reality?

The clinical perspective deriving from Lacanian ethics considers pathology in terms of desire. If the philosophical premise is that reality is a symbolic construction, with the ethical implication that one must take responsibility for creating one's reality, then the consequent clinical perspective examines psychical distress as a function of the desire (successful or not) behind the structuring of reality. Depression, for instance, can then be viewed as a condition marked by lack of desire, while anxiety—or in Lacanian terms *anguish*—as a condition of either unclear or repressed desire. Symptoms are unconscious representational modes of desire. In Lacanian ethics, the analyst again and again enquires into desire: Do you live according to the desire that inhabits you (Lacan, 1992 [1959], p. 60)? This is not an ethics that envisions normalcy, adaptation, choosing the golden mean, socialisation, achievement or living up to others' expectations. Nor does it seek serenity, ascesis or religiosity of any kind. Since there is no complete "free choice" as any choice is subject to unconscious conditions, emphasis here, rather than on a person's desire, is on the—often unconscious—desire within him, the desire that owns him. The objective of treatment is to elicit the patient's internal agency of unconscious choice and to help him identify with it, enabling him eventually to say: "In view of the actions that flow from the unconscious—this is my will!" This agency is one of the meanings of the Lacanian notion of the subject of the unconscious.

This is why the Lacanian psychoanalyst is alert to any signs of unconscious wishes in the patient's speech. When the latter tells him he is late because he had a hard time leaving his computer game, the psychoanalyst will relate to his late coming as an expression of desire arising during play. Rather than conscious statements of the type "I wanted to arrive in time", a person's will is expressed in those parts of his speech where desire appears without conscious intention: "I had a hard time leaving the computer."[2] While desire was embodied in the acting out of the late arrival, it was interpreted and formulated only in terms of the conversation about the reasons for this lateness.

The patient's subject of the unconscious is extracted and identified too, moreover, by means of the role construction in the clinic. In the reality of the clinic, the psychoanalyst positions himself as object—wanted, loved, and object of the patient's transference relations—with the aim to prompt the patient to take a subject position—loving, and with a will that takes possession of the therapeutic space.

This however should not lead us to ignore the fact that the psychoanalyst, too, is a desiring subject, and that this desire is inseparable from his ethical position and his analytic work. Hence the chapter dedicated to ethics also deals with the desire of the psychoanalyst. What desires however should inform and direct the psychoanalyst in his encounter with the patient? What desire can the psychoanalyst entertain if he occupies the object position in the relationship? If treatment aims to draw out the subject and understand it, then how is the psychoanalyst, having undergone analysis himself, to position himself as object? This is a paradoxical desire: it is easier to determine what it isn't than what it is. Society's normative values, for instance, are not fundamentally the psychoanalyst's desire (Lacan, 1988 [1953], pp. 222–223). Nor does the search for factual truth, which motivated Freud, stimulate the psychoanalyst's desire according to Lacan. The analytic object of desire is the use of the Symbolic dimension, the medium of speech in treatment, for the sake of producing effects in the Real, that is, so as to achieve actual change in the patient's modes of desire and jouissance. This is a desire that recalls the poet's wish to arouse feelings and effect changes in the world by means of words. It is a very specific and paradoxical desire to embody the object of desire. Functioning as object, the psychoanalyst stirs the patient to become subject and express his desires.

Chapter Two looks at how the various elements of the ritual-symbolic space—including time, money, furniture, the handshake—are managed to support the treatment. Reference is made to the following questions: How does one set the first appointment? What's especially important in the first meetings? How does one conduct oneself in the role of the one who is assumed to know, the one asked: "Tell me, what's my problem?" How does one accept being hated, or admired and loved, without identifying with these roles? Other questions discussed are: What's the point of free association in the treatment? How can one prompt it? And once the associations come, how to make sure they keep coming? How does one listen? To what? How does one ask questions? And how does one interpret? What to do with a patient's slips of the tongue? And what about one's own? Is every mistake a Freudian mistake? Why use a couch? How to make the transition from chair to couch? In Lacanian psychoanalysis, it is the analyst who determines the length of each session through an act called *cutting the session*. Why should a session be cut? And how is this achieved? What are the theoretical objections to cutting sessions?

In addition, Chapter Two also deals with the psychoanalyst's starting position. He does not expect the patient to copy him or identify with him, and he should take an ironical stance regarding his own prejudice (in other words: not to identify with his own preconceptions). He must moreover opt for a non-judgmental attitude where it concerns his patient's impulses: he should not be shocked or put off by the things he hears. This is a position he can take, among other things, as a result of his own psychoanalysis where he has come to recognise all these impulses also inside himself. Such a position of human solidarity, on the basis of recognising one's own drives, is one of the key reasons why psychoanalysis is a crucial part of analytic training.

Chapter Three deals with the transference. What is transference? How is it managed? What does the psychoanalyst do with the patient's demands? What is one to do when the transference is positive? And what when the transference is negative? The basic assumption is that the engine of the transference, and the treatment, is the psychoanalyst's showing the patient his desire as something for which the latter is responsible.

Further questions discussed in this chapter are: How to apply the theoretical principle according to which the psychoanalyst serves as object, or more specifically, as what Lacan called "the object that serves as the cause of desire"? How is the treatment to be conducted in such a manner that the psychoanalyst acts as a moving force driving the patient to act in his life? How to deal with the patient's resistance to letting go of jouissance and to knowing his desire (i.e., the removal of repression)?[3] How is one to forge the transition from perceiving the subject's symptoms as an outcome of his history (i.e., a biographical approach) to seeing them as a style enabling jouissance and desire (i.e., a structural approach)?

Chapter Four approaches the question of the nature of the symptom, and of the difference between psychic and medical symptom. If for Descartes, existence was predicated on thought ("I think therefore I am"), for Lacan, it is predicated on desire ("I desire therefore I am"). Accordingly, the symptom is the subject's unconscious way of maintaining desire, that is, to exist as a subject. Does this mean that "I suffer therefore I am"? Not quite. The suffering which Freud called "neurotic" originates in alienation from the symptom, as though it wasn't part of the subject. If, however, the subject identifies with his desire, which is maintained by the symptom, then his suffering from the symptom will decrease significantly. In treatment, some symptoms will cease, while the patient will identify with others. The chapter also discusses the role in psychoanalysis of the analytic symptom (a symptom perceived as being caused by the treatment or appearing in the course of the treatment, though it wasn't what the patient complained of initially). Also discussed is the nature of the relations between symptom—as said, a way to exist as a desiring subject—and phantasm, which is a way to obtain pleasure.

Chapter Five addresses common problems in psychoanalytic treatment, first of all anxiety, or anguish in Lacanian terms, a widespread psychic phenomenon for which Lacanian theory offers a unique clinical approach. Here the questions discussed are: How is one to extract desire and jouissance from the anguish in which they are enfolded, thus to reduce the attendant distress? How does one work with depression; with suicidal tendencies; with trauma? How to work with the unconscious materials arising from dreams or nightmares? How can one make sense of impulsive behaviours, and are they a message that needs deciphering?

Chapter Six deals with diagnosis in relation to three clinical structures: psychosis, perversion, and neurosis—the latter of which is divided into an obsessive structure and a hysterical structure. Questions discussed are: How does each of these structures relate to the oedipal complex? How do these structures serve as a strategy of desire for the subject? How does the psychoanalyst specifically attune his work and his presence to these diverse structures? How to conduct an effective diagnosis on the basis of the patient's attitude to issues like time, space, transference, the law, desire, and jouissance?

The final chapter, Chapter Seven, is dedicated to termination of the treatment. It proposes a distinction between psychoanalytically based psychotherapy and psychoanalysis. While the former's main objective is the reduction of mental suffering, coming to an end when symptoms pass, the latter also offers an investigation of the unconscious, the impulses, the relations between history and personality—an investigation crucial to the psychoanalyst's training. Since psychoanalysis is not only a treatment method but also a training method for the psychoanalyst, the final chapter is simultaneously an introduction to the first chapter, which dealt with the psychoanalyst's position. The question that marks termination of the analysis is: "Have you lived the desire that inhabits you?"

This book, unless otherwise stated, refers to work with neurotic patients. It deals only sporadically with work with psychotic patients, and even less with Lacan's late thinking, which touches on work with Real jouissance, beyond language, and which refers to Oedipus and the clinical structures as a Freudian myth that can be transcended. These topics lend themselves less easily to discussion, certainly not for readers who are not very familiar with the basics, with Freud's writings and with Lacan's early writings. I hope this book casts light on questions concerning psychoanalytic practice; stirs readers' desire to study psychoanalysis, and makes its contribution to the conservation of the corpus of psychoanalytic knowledge.

CHAPTER ONE

Ethical foundations

Ontology—anti-essentialism and a desire-based reality

For Lacan things do not have an essence as such—an approach whose core can already be perceived in Freud's writings. Lacan points out the fundamentally anti-essentialist spirit first manifests in Freud's *Beyond the Pleasure Principle* (1920g). While in the case of animals, gratification only occurs once food is actually digested, humans can actually transform the absence of nourishment (hunger, that is), into an entity in its own right by means of statements like: "I am hungry." While, in other words, for animals, absence only presents itself as absence (and presence as presence), language makes it possible for humans to make something present even when it is absent. Lacan's anti-essentialism is directly associated with the central role he ascribed to language in the formation of the psyche, and especially to this particular quality of language, namely its ability to turn nothing into something, what lacks actuality into a symbolic-conceptual entity (Lacan, 1992 [1959], p. 187).

Anti-essentialism is not a new way of thinking. Heraclitus, the pre-Socratic philosopher, argued that one cannot enter the same river twice because its water is in constant flux (so that on our next dip, it cannot be the same). In addition, the person who enters the river a second time

1

will never be quite the same as on the previous occasion, since she or he too changes constantly. This is the logic Lacan adopts—but he explains that even if one cannot enter the same river twice, or indeed even once, where it comes to the river *qua* concept, it can be entered again and again. Thus, we can enter "the Jordan river" time and again. It is conceptualisations like "Jordan river" that create the illusion of essence.

This principle of conceptualisation—or signification, in Lacan's terminology—is what allows experiential continuity and object permanence. Similarly, continuity and permanence also form the basis of the clinical phenomenon Freud called repetition compulsion (which is why Lacan attributes what Freud identified as repetition compulsion to language as a system of signifiers) (Efrati & Israely, 2007, p. 62). During her treatment, one patient said: "I'm having a hard time adjusting to this foreign culture. Something about it doesn't suit me." In subsequent free associations, she talked about how she hadn't fitted in with her high school's floor gymnastics team because she was too tall, and how her mother had commented about something she embroidered, when she was a girl: "That doesn't fit." Some of the cultural misfit this patient experiences due to being an immigrant is influenced by the repetition of the charged signifier in her mother's criticism: "That doesn't fit." Repetition, in other words, is based on signifiers ("doesn't fit" or "inappropriate", in this case). For Lacan, a signifier is any mode of representation—whether an expression, a word, or even an icon—and its meaning he calls signified.[1]

The Freudian unconscious, it is important to note, rather than an organic entity, is a system of meanings that have become repressed as a result of the wish not to know. There are various autonomous systems that are responsible for physiological functions like intestinal activity, heartrate, sleep regulation—and about which we might say that they are not conscious, but these are of no interest to psychoanalysis. Though it is obviously possible to reduce mental suffering by non-verbal means (whether through medication or through alternative methods), the Freudian unconscious is inextricably bound up with language, and hence the work of Lacanian treatment is work with words (Lacan, 2002 [1964a], p. 703).

This anti-essentialism implies that every patient is intimately and specifically involved in the perception of their own reality. Lacan adopts Descartes' notion that reality is not self-evident—reflected in his famous dictum "I think therefore I am" or rather "I doubt therefore I am".

Following Freud, however, Lacan—unlike Descartes—sees existence validated through desire rather than by means of thought ("I desire therefore I am") (Lacan, 1966). It is through the symptom that the subject maintains desire while not identifying it as such. Thus, for instance, a patient who suffers from being looked at wishes not to acknowledge her own exhibitionist desire.

This approach raises the following question: What reality do the symptoms of which the patient complains constitute? It transpired, for instance, that a patient who was suffering from chronic fatigue and sleeping many hours each day had heard from his mother, early in his life, that he looked just like a prince when asleep. In his unconscious the reality of sleep turns him into a prince. Or, in other words: the desire to be a prince produces a symptomatic reality of chronic fatigue. Dreams are another site where reality bases itself on desire. If a patient dreams she enters a labyrinth in the course of her morning run and doesn't manage to get out of it, one may assume that in the dream she creates a reality in which it is impossible to run—because she's trying to find a way out of running. Treating the spraining of a foot during a run as a Freudian bungled action reflects a similar logic.

The manner in which desire shapes reality is well illustrated by the phenomenon of depression. Someone who experiences depression feels that she or he is losing out on something. What is it that they are missing? Depression is a state in which desire is absent. Since desire requires the absence of a gratifying object (absence, that is), depression is a state in which the absence necessary for desire is not available. The paradox in depression is that the absence required for desire is absent. The depressed person, then, loses the possibility to live with loss, that is with lack, with desire. Whereas animals take pleasure in what actually is present– they are gratified, reach homeostasis, by eating or sleeping, for instance—humans, given as they are to language, also seek the satisfaction offered by hunger—linguistically signified by the word "appetite". Appetite and yearning are real for us. This is how mankind distinguishes itself from animals, according to Lacan. While the pleasure principle is responsible for the animal gratification associated with satiety, which originates in the consumption of a real object, satisfaction in the order of yearning—beyond the pleasure principle—is realised by virtue of language. "At last I'm having an appetite again. I had absolutely no appetite when I was depressed"—these are the words of someone whose attitude to lack has recovered by means of the recovery of her or his linkage to language-reality. The latter allows for satisfaction from living, beyond the animal gratification achieved by eating and sleeping. So, for instance when a depressed person grows angry, this should be considered a certain demandingness that involves desire. Interpretation then should release the demand that the anger holds and, subsequently, the desire held by the demand. Anger as it were signals a burgeoning sense of hunger. When all goes well, this hunger will evolve into an appetite, into a desire for life. If we take a didactic position, assuming that anger is a way of avoiding responsibility, we'll miss the opportunity to channel this anger beyond the pleasure principle, in other words: to extract the potential for desire from within anger.

To Freud, the positivist, for whom the dream was less real than waking life and thus opened the door to unconscious fantasy, the dream seemed the royal road to the unconscious. As for Lacan, the postmodernist, reality too takes the shape of an illusion. The non-mediated actuality of existence, according to him, manifests itself at rare moments only, for instance on waking, only in order then to become submerged in a multitude of identifications grounded in concepts and images (Lacan, 1966). Hence Lacan believes that speech no less than the dream is an inroad to the unconscious.

The validity of reality

Where, then, originates the feeling that reality necessarily exists and that it is accessible? If the word (or signifier) does not fully describe the thing and mainly generates meaning, then where does the illusion of full representation derive? Freud and Lacan had different answers to this question. While Freud's point of departure was his work with neurotic patients, Lacan began his psychoanalytic career with patients who were psychotic. Psychosis even more urgently raises the question of participation in reality—the case of delusions is a good example. What is it that neurotic patients have, unlike psychotic patients, and that allows them to take part in a common reality? Could it be some shared delusion? What's that wink of those who're in on the secret, that the psychotic person doesn't get? The function enabling this participation in reality, Lacan calls the "Name of the Father" (Lacan, 1992 [1955], p. 193). The Name of the Father is a very particular signifier whose very meaning is that signifiers carry meanings. The recorded laughter in American TV comedies, for instance, constitutes a signifier that tells spectators: "This is a funny joke and you should laugh now." The Name of the Father, on similar lines, is, as it were, the zero-commandment that stipulates that the following Ten Commandments are meaningful.

This function, validating reality as something that has existence, works overtime in the case of neurotic people. Neurotics, we might even say, take reality religiously. They ardently believe in reality. They hold tight onto reality and say: "This exists!" "This is!" In the case of an obsessive neurosis, for instance, the compulsive urge to touch certain objects (doorknobs, for instance) can be understood as a way of finding release from the virtual, symbolic aspect of reality (by taking hold of an actual object). Typical symptoms of hysterical neurosis—like the urge to take centre stage, to be seen—come to counteract the fragility of reality in so far as it is reinforced by the gaze by the following logic: "I am seen therefore I am."

Neurotic individuals have very little access to reality's basic foundation. Those suffering from psychosis, by contrast, lacking that foundation, know that they somehow fail to get the wink of those who are in on the secret, and are therefore aware of the existence of a common secret. This wink, which is transparent to neurotic people who are convinced that reality is one and the same thing as actuality—this wink is alien to psychotic patients, who are therefore aware of the language bond in which they are not included. Psychotic people can, nevertheless, dwell in reality by joining a social structure that is maintained by others. A patient with a psychotic personality structure will be too shy to phone a girl whom he would like to get to know, except when he is in the building where the clinic he attends is also located. It is only under the actual protection of the Other[2] that he is capable of using the function of the Name of the Father by way of a key to conducting himself in the Symbolic order of reality. Other with a capital O is the English rendering of the French *Autre* which refers to the other (Other) not as equal but as authority.

As opposed to neurotic people who cannot disengage themselves from reality (about whose Imaginary and Symbolic nature, as mentioned, they do not know), and as opposed to psychotic people who cannot take a hold on it—people with perversions play with reality. And they most particularly play with the tension between the existence and the absence of the foundations of reality, the name of the father. Thus, the one who's playing knows what the other doesn't: the reality in which the latter lives is illusory, and the conditions validating the reality of the one who's being played with, and which allow them to believe in the game, are controlled by the one who plays. This is how the one who plays upholds reality while knowing it's an illusion. Between the player and the object of her or his play the reality is alternatingly confirmed and denied. Perverse individuals use the law to confirm reality. The function of the Name of the Father that validates reality is supported in the case of perverse structure by the presence of the law. In order to summon the law that supports the validity of language they need to break the law. So that in perverse logic, the crime makes the law appear as broken, and once the law exists reality is validated.

Lacan's view of reality as an invention does not leave clinical work untouched. The fact that the psychoanalyst interprets validates—for Lacan—the assumption that there is something to be interpreted: that there is an unconscious. The unconscious too is a conceptualisation in language. Slips were not Freudian until Freud referred to them as such. When the psychoanalyst reflects about a Freudian slip, she produces a reality in which unconscious desires are associated with the patient's symptoms. Psychoanalytic discourse establishes a reality and sub-realities in order to allow for therapeutic analytical effects (Lacan, 1966).

This reality-generating mechanism operates by means of a logic of "afterwardsness" (*Nachträglichkeit*). In simple positivist logic, an existing phenomenon (say, the existence of God) entails certain consequences (for instance, the ritual of prayers). According to the logic of afterwardsness, the outcome is what produces the reason: prayer maintains the assumption that God exists. Gods come into existence by the observance of their injunctions. The assumed reality produces itself in hindsight. From a positivist perspective—which thinks of symptoms as the result of an *a-priori* reality—one may argue that a man is lacking in confidence because his father died when he was very young. The Lacanian view, postulating that it is the symptom that creates the reality, allows us to think of the symptom of lack of confidence as a way for the patient to position himself "below" the confident father. The patient creates a structure including an authority figure to whom he is subjected, and his lack of confidence allows him to maintain this structure. That is to say, due to the symptom of insecurity a patient keeps hold of the dead father as though he were alive (the same father without whom there is no security).

When a child says something clever that causes the grown-ups to laugh he will repeat it on other occasions in order to make people laugh.

The annals of his memory will record that he told a joke, even though what he said, when he did so for the first time, was not meant to provoke hilarity. On similar lines, it is only once we have reacted to a Freudian slip as something enfolding an unconscious desire—i.e., only once we refer to the slip as Freudian—that we can conclude there is an unconscious desire.

This motivation to adopt such a position, according to which reality is an invention, underlies the ethics of subject formation. People with neurosis identify themselves with their mirror image as if reality prescribed it. Psychoanalysts try to slightly shift the mirror so they may become aware of its existence, thus to understand that they're dealing with a mere reflection. We want to unsettle their fanatic faith in reality so as to help them evolve an ambiguous space in which they stand out as subjects who decide between meanings. In the work with psychotic patients whose reality is fragile and consists of a patchwork of delusions, our effort will be the opposite: to help them participate in a common reality. In the case of psychotic patients, the aim is exactly to generate a shared (and therefore less delusional) patch in those places where reality is without roots or foundation. Here, then, substantiating identity or defining one's aim in life are actually appropriate therapeutic objectives. The aim of treatment is to consolidate a reality in which patients can function as subjects. We, as psychoanalysts, are part of the structure that maintains them as subjects.

Ambiguity and subject position

Emerging as a result of conceptualisations, reality is not actual and this means that it is not unambiguous either. Rather than objective factors it is the desire of the subject that dictates reality perception, and this desire involves deliberation at sites of vagueness or ambiguity. Since it is through such decision making that the subject comes into being, we try, in clinical work with patients suffering from neurosis, to make an appeal to (or to make present) the one who is responsible for choosing, for creating the reality, where reality seems objective. One way of doing this is by directing attention to the ambiguities in patients' words, a code that requires deciphering, on the lines of the Freudian slip which holds a secret. That it is possible to decide how we understand or perceive the meaning of a word is an opportunity to bring to bear desire. One can offer patients the interpretation that their choice for one meaning rather than another is evidence of their desire, thus suggesting their existence as subjects who make choices.

To illustrate this, take a patient who says: "I am off putting" by which he consciously intends to say that he is "disgusting". The analyst, by asking "… putting it off to another time?", suggests the ambiguity of the statement (he might here be identifying a theme in the patient's way of talking). Exposing the ambiguity comes to allow the patient to raise his unconscious desire to the surface (which in this case may express itself in a refusal to stick to appointments).

Still, in principle, meaning can be interpreted endlessly: Another meaning can always be found, but this may undermine the effort to make subjectivity present. Dwelling on all possible meanings is tantamount to sitting on the fence in terms of one's desires. Cutting the session (see the subsection, below, on this issue) at the point of one meaning is the same as cutting it at the point of one wish. Desire is the wish for the sake of whose realisation one is willing to give up on other wishes. For desire to be what it is, it does not have to be realised. But it does exact a price or an effort, the foregoing of some meanings or other desires. This is why the psychoanalyst sometimes halts the slippage of meanings by linking signifier with signified, word and meaning (through cutting a session, for instance). This type of linking, Lacan calls it *capitonnage* (buttoning or quilting), stabilises the reality of the patient's desire. Here the psychoanalyst actually goes with a certain meaning, relying on her judgment of the choice made by the patient's unconscious (sometimes, therefore, she might take the initiative to end a meeting).

Lack of ambiguity is a hallmark of fascism or perversion, which are typically free of the burden of choice. Ambiguity, then, is on one line with an anti-fascist reality (liberation from the tyranny of the great Imaginary Other, as will transpire below) (Lacan, 1974),—a reality that can be considered in terms of creativity. So, for instance, the power of the poetic text is associated with the fact that it never holds out one clear meaning. Hence, in the work with people with neurosis, the objective is to reduce the hold of their belief in the language-culture-meaning system which Lacan calls the "Other"—without however arrogating the place of this Other (for instance by preaching rejection of that Other). When working with psychotic individuals any interpretation touching on ambiguity may precipitate a psychotic attack, since they are only tenuously linked into the system of the Other. Once the validity of the system comes under question delusions may arise which are aimed to create an Other, like the God whom the psychotic patient serves as his messiah.

Loss of the object as a condition for desire

If reality is made up of objects, and if an object is an event that has been singularised and defined by means of a signifier or even the creation *ex nihilo* of a reality following the signifier; and if what determines the way the world is divided into objects and their creation is the subject's unconscious desire—then one might argue that the signifier rather than describing the actual object, creates it. Hence, if it is possible to speak about a representational function in the context of the signifier, then the created object does not describe a reality but rather points at the existence of its creator. The object of representation is the subject. The signifier, in its manifold meanings, represents the subject who is required to adjudicate between them (Lacan, 1961, session 1).

A paradigmatic formulation of the Lacanian myth of the subject's birth into the order of reality is the child's passage from demanding gratification from her mother (*qua* object) to calling the latter by her name. It is this call, speech—the use, that is, of signifiers—that constitutes the speaker as a desiring subject. Concurrently with the loss of the real lost object (one of whose manifestations, as said, is the mother's full and comforting presence) a satisfiable need comes into being as well as a demand that cannot be satisfied. While the need for the mother's milk can be fulfilled, this is not the case where it comes to security, love and the guaranteed infinite supply of milk. This type of security is the forever lost object. The search for it yields an incessant stream of alternatives (not one object successfully replaces the demand that surfaced upon the loss of the mythological object). This constant turnover of objects constitutes the subject in the Symbolic domain. The clinical structures of psychosis, perversion, and—obsessive and hysterical—neurosis, first formulated by Freud and taken on by Lacan, are demarcated by their different way of coping with object loss.

For Lacan, this loss is crucial in the establishment of subjectivity, because with every lost object the subject experiences more of the drive that ties her or him to reality. By this logic, the oral drive for instance is associated with the lost nipple. Loss, therefore, is the condition for the emergence of any urge or yearning. This way of thinking will profoundly affect the manner in which we listen to our patients' complaints. We will not consider their demand for a reduction in our fees or their grumbling about their spouses as concrete lack which has to be met with an object. Rather than asking ourselves, "How can we help her to feel satisfied?" we will wonder, "What desire does this complaint express, and how does it constitute her as a subject?"

A young patient, for instance, who doesn't manage to choose a professional course, complains about the education system. One might think he doesn't like the idea of becoming an educator, but his complaint about the "disappearance of good education" can also be heard as giving expression to how important education is for him—that is, to his desire to educate. Patients, at times, cannot express their desire other than by means of a complaint ("Why can't we meet at the time I wanted?" "Why can't you reduce your fee for me?"). Meeting the demand will only up the ante, claims Lacan, it's simple: in meeting the patient's request we actually disappoint his expectation for us to come up with an interpretation that identifies his desire (the desire concealed by the request to pay a reduced fee may be his desire to be loved). Meeting the demand is tantamount to a kind of refusal to understand, an unwillingness to find out the desire behind this demand, while according to Lacanian ethical understanding means the identification of desire. When desire is met—by means not of gratification but through acknowledgement—the demand becomes attenuated. Thus, in couple therapy sometimes all it takes is both partners' recognition of each other's wishes, even if they don't satisfy them. Once there is such recognition, which usually comes with a great sense of relief, they won't find it hard to reach some form of compromise.

The registers of the Real, the Imaginary, and the Symbolic

Lacan approaches the reality of the subject in terms of the relations among three registers. The register of the Real refers to the world as such, unfiltered. This is not the physical Real but that of human experience. The experience of the Real, of actual existence, is by definition unmediated by representation (whether Imaginary or Symbolic)—it breaks boundaries and floods the subject. Such infraction happens for instance in traumatic situations, when words and concepts collapse under the strain of actual events, and equally in states of ecstasy. When a person is seriously injured, for example, we stop seeing her in terms of the intact body. When the human figure disintegrates and the flesh is exposed, or the inner organs, one realises that the body's integrity was always illusory anyhow. Professionals like doctors or nurses or emergency workers are more protected against the traumatic irruption of the Real by their technical-professional terminology. When phenomena enter language—undergo symbolisation, that is—the Real is tamed and the whole figure or words are restored: this is re-presentation.

The Imaginary register evolves from the subject's identification with the image of her or his body as a gestalt. This register is not specific to the individual person. It is common to many animals for the image of the body of their own species to arouse sexual and violent instincts. Lacan conceptualised the "mirror stage" as the logical moment when the baby brings together its mirror image with itself. This identification is mediated by the parents who symbolically confirm it when they exclaim: "That's you!" (Lacan, 1988 [1954], p. 50).

The child's real, pre-Imaginary experience is one of fragmentation. The child envies the grown-ups who are in control of their body parts while she lacks coordination. Discovering her parents' object of love in her mirror image, she falls in love with her own image (in obvious paraphrase of the myth of Narcissus who falls in love with his own reflected image). This mirror image constitutes the ego's essence. The moment of self-identification with her image, with the emergent ego in her own shape, is vital to her ability to relate to herself as distinct from her surroundings. And it is equally vital for sexual attraction in so far as it results from visual appearance. Aggression and hate, too, appear in the Imaginary register. Experiencing herself as fragmented, the child envies her whole image and develops rivalry towards it. In so far as the other, too, has outlines that define him, he incorporates this reflection. Treatment with persons with neurosis aims to weaken the ego's tight hold on them—a hold Lacan refers to as a miss-identification (neurotic people's identification with their own image)—in order for them to identify with their will, which is directed outward, not at their self-image, which is the other's object of love. This is the transition from being wanted to actively wanting.

In the Symbolic register the reference is to language, signifiers, and social systems—which are also grounded in signifiers and laws, in symbols and roles. Language is the medium through which humans engage in social relations and it forms the groundworks of their thinking and their unconscious action alike. Being external and internal at one and the same time, the Symbolic register undoes the imaginary distinction between inside and outside. Desires (ostensibly internal) are actually circulated among people by means of language. There is no desiring outside the frame of what has been marked as valuable by the other. This is what led Lacan to observe: "Desire is the desire of the other." Any notion of independent desire rests only in an imaginary fiction of autonomy. In psychoanalysis especially, the Symbolic register takes a prominent place because psychoanalysis aims to ameliorate suffering by diverting imaginary identification (identification as a figure for the other) to make more place for symbolic identification (identification as having desire).

One of the treatment's main efforts is directed at getting the patient to speak, revealing momentous signifiers (like for instance "inappropriate"), allowing the subject to be set free, to some extent, from their grip. Like the narrative approach in psychotherapy, psychoanalysis too associates between meanings and suffering, but while the former attempts to alter the constellation of signifiers and to reframe the narrative by which the patient lives, Lacanian psychoanalysis attributes change to scrutinising one's very motivation for telling oneself a certain story—a motivation which leaves its imprint on the meaning of the chosen signifiers. That is to say: while the narrative approach replaces one signifier with another, psychoanalysis hopes to alter the meaning of the signifier (which is no other than the signified). Such change occurs as a result of zooming in on signifiers in a manner that raises questions about alternative meanings. Such a preoccupation is likely to tease out the desire and jouissance these meanings hold, and reflection on other signifiers is likely to evacuate some of their heavy charge.

The Other—with a capital O—is either Imaginary or Symbolic. In its Imaginary aspect, the Other is a despot with whom the subject is locked in a sado-masochistic dyad. Often, especially at the beginning of treatment, patients tend to see their parents through this prism and themselves as their parents' victims. The Symbolic Other, by contrast, is impersonal; rather it is the system itself. When the patient understands that his parents are subject to the same human limitations (including the influence of their own parents) he has the opportunity to abandon the victim position and to embrace at least some part of his fate. It is therefore useful for the treatment to cover at least a three-generation segment of the lineage continuum. This approach may help patients extract themselves from the Imaginary perspective of dualism in order to perceive the generational chain of desires, encoded in signi-fiers and constituting them as subjects. Rather than seeing the parent as the oppressive Other, they can now think of her as subject, just like themselves, to intergenerational transference, which is precisely what makes up the Symbolic Other.

Another concept that functions differentially in the Symbolic register and in the Imaginary, is castration. Imaginary castration is concrete—the loss of the penis brought about by the Imaginary (or figurative) father: the prohibition to gratify desire. Symbolic castration, by contrast, is not conducted by a specific figure and does not concern the actual body. It occurs as the subject emerges on the signifier's entry into the living creature's existence, when the baby begins using language as alterna-tive gratification for things, and words divide the world into objects for him (Lacan, 1988 [1954], p. 156). If castration's Imaginary meaning puts a clamp on pleasure, Symbolic castration is the very origin of desire. The symbolically castrating Other is language, which is always attended by a dissatisfaction about words not being things. This dissatisfaction forms the basis of human desire. Having borrowed the notion of cas-tration from Freud, by drawing the distinction between the Imaginary and the Symbolic register, Lacan however highlighted the necessity of castration for human development.

Ethics

Ethics is a conceptualisation of the good life—an answer to the question how it is right and proper to live. Does the ethics of Lacanian treatment aim for happiness? In his essay "Culture and its discontents" (1930a), Freud says explicitly that he does not believe in happiness as either possibility or objective (Freud, 1930a, p. 89). For him, nothing makes a person more miserable than a belief in happiness, when not attained. One aim of psychoanalysis is to shake off the thought of the neighbour's greener grass. The most obvious illustration of neurotic misery is the envy of another, better, yet missed sexuality. This variation on penis envy is the actual core of neurosis. Happiness prevails when rather than the objective (especially the failed objective), it is the by-product of striving to attain another goal, the by-product, that is, of yearning. In the treatment, on similar lines, a symptom may be resolved provided its resolution is not the objective. When we listen to the patient with the aim to make space for her or his desires rather than to reduce their pain, the symptom, which is after all nothing but an awkward expression of desire, becomes superfluous in its present form.

By the same logic, analytic treatment, most definitely does not aim to attain an insight or philosophical illumination as such, as some critics of psychoanalysis presume: It looks for the reduction of suffering. The ethics of Lacanian psychoanalysis however is based on the assumption that where there is attention to desire suffering will be reduced. Psychoanalysis' paradoxical approach to treating pain indirectly evolved from a recognition of the paradoxical nature of pleasure. Lacanian theory differentiates desire from pleasure. Pleasure has a limit, and when this limit is exceeded suffering arises. The notion of jouissance refers to excess pleasure which therefore is accompanied by suffering. The ethics of happiness is an ethics of the pursuit of maximum pleasure which, paradoxically, issues in the suffering caused by crossing the boundary of pleasure (Lacan, 1978 [1963], p. 183).

The absence of jouissance is of course likely to be destructive, as is the case in certain types of depression. But as absolute jouissance is no less destructive, Lacanian treatment stresses the formation of a subjectivity that is grounded in yearning. Rather than biological mechanisms describing an organic dynamic of addiction, destructive jouissance is about the human fantasy of unlimited, unrestricted happiness. The more independent the subject becomes of the fantasy of fullness, and the more any residual lack takes the form of desire (in marked contrast with depression), the less addicted she becomes to jouissance with its inevitable suffering. In an ethics that is characterised by the pursuit of objectives—like for instance happiness—yearning is perceived as a frustration, the result of non-achievement, rather than as vitality.

Paradoxically, it is a utilitarian ethic that opposes wasteful jouissance that may well end up in excess—as in the case of the symptom of workaholism—that an uncontrolled eruption of jouissance is likely to occur, as the latter breaks free of the utilitarian plan which stipulates that there must be a rhyme and reason for everything. These are the situations when we hear the patient say: "I do things but I don't know why I am doing them." While at times, it may be possible to find a reason, often the conclusion will be that the absence of a reason may well be the very reason; that the absence of meaning is the very meaning of being free of meaning. Lacanian ethics in this sense resembles the ethics of the way, of the Chinese *Dao*. Once the subject is no longer frustrated, because she realises that the objective is a fantasy, she may enjoy yearning. Lacan mentions Sufi mystics' ability to take pleasure in their desire (Lacan, 1961, session 25).

Kantian ethics however he identifies with the ethics of Sade due to their shared ambition for a maximum universal jouissance to be achieved by injunctions. While Sade insists on everybody's right to take pleasure in one another, Kant's imperative forbids jouissance altogether. Kant's argument is that when we all sacrifice our jouissance for the sake of that of the other, jouissance's gross national product, as it were, will be optimal. Sade, by contrast, taking a capitalist approach, argues that the GNP of jouissance can be maximised if everybody is allowed to pursue unlimited jouissance. As far as Lacan is concerned, both subscribe to an ethics of imperative, and neither of them believes in desire, only in jouissance (Lacan, 1992 [1959], p. 70).

Kant's position, Lacan identifies with obsessive neurosis, while he considers that of Sade to be on a line with perversion. For Lacan, the injunction to take pleasure is a function of the super-ego. Though we usually associate the super-ego with the prohibition of pleasure, Lacan explains that the very notion of the injunction is at the core of the super-ego. "You owe it to yourself," it says in an advertisement for manicure. Here is the super-ego commanding that one take pleasure. Freud too commented on the jouissance enfolded in the very act of prohibition. The cruelty of the super-ego resides in its denial of pleasure, but it is precisely in this cruelty that the pleasure of the id inheres, under the cover up of the judge's robe, as it were. The function of the super-ego rests fundamentally on jouissance regardless of the injunction's direction—in favour of jouissance or against it. Patients who are crushed by their super-ego to the point of severe depression, frequently report on the pleasure they derive from "snuggling up" with their depression. Once a patient comes to concretely understand how the activity of the super-ego serves as jouissance, all it will take is to tell her "You're really indulging yourself too much" by way of interpreting her persistent guilt.

The super-ego that commands to take pleasure, Freud called the "maternal super-ego"; Lacan, however, showed how jouissance is attached to every aspect of the super-ego, whether it's sadistic abuse in the guise of morality or the masochism of guilt, or in the direct form of the injunction to take pleasure. There is also a cultural-historical aspect to the conversion of the command to avoid pleasure into a command to take pleasure. The same is true for how the drives are defined. Unlike in Freud's times, almost every form of jouissance is currently legal and normative; consensual sex between adults embraces almost every possibility. The contemporary super-ego functions rather as an injunction to sexual pleasure. This is more obvious among the younger patients: the injunction is to go out as much as possible, get excited— even if one doesn't really feel like it. The US comics artist Bill Griffith captured this very well when he makes his hero, Zippy Pinhead, ask— "Are we having fun yet?"—a question that has become a standing joke in America.[3]

The super-ego in its pleasure-negating quality is nowadays mainly articulated in relation to what we eat. The cult of the body image recruits the super-ego to prohibit the pleasure of eating. This is reflected in the large choice of diets available and the epidemic of eating disorders.

Jouissance's paradoxical nature (both supported as well as negated by the injunction) flies in the face of the philosophical groundworks of many ethical approaches. Sade's ethics seeks to create a catastrophic collapse, to be followed by a new creation. Lacan argues that Sade understood something Kant did not see about the relations between the death drive and creativity. Creation is a sublimation of the death drive and involves catastrophe. Prometheus is by no means alone in offering mankind a gift that includes destruction—especially the destruction of himself. The South American myths concerning the origins of human achievements and discoveries (e.g., the use of stones and fire for cooking) collected by Claude Levi-Strauss recount a catastrophic event, usually involving incest. Incest is a universal image of ecstatic, unbounded pleasure leading to devastation, the disappearance of the circumscribed self as a result of fusion with the mother. The moment of creation, like the moment of birth, is a passage from fusion to separation.

Another dichotomising ethics can be found in existentialism. It is grounded in a simple division between inside and outside, and free human beings are viewed, as in Rousseau, as those who rid themselves of the chains of the social structure. Lacan's logic regarding the relation between subject and language, the social-symbolic structure, is both more complex and more paradoxical. For Lacan each entails the other. To illustrate this relationship, Lacan refers to the topological shape of the Möbius strip in which the dichotomy between inside and outside, now situated on one continuum, vanishes.

Figure 1. The Moebius strip. Illustration courtesy of Resling Publishers, Israel. Israely, Y. (2014). "The Craft of Lacanian Treatment". Tel-Aviv Israel: Resling. p. 41 (In Hebrew).

If we place humankind and society, both, on the sequence of the Möbius strip, we can argue that the subject does not exist other than as a function of the social structure. This construal undoes the myth about the tension between individual and society as something that can be resolved. Individual responsibility, on this approach, does not aim for liberation from social frameworks but for the cultivation of a new attitude to them (which, in turn, might change them, and so on). The Symbolic domain which Rousseau believes hems in human beings, is the very foundation of humanity for Lacan, the grounds of subjecthood, and it offers the context for all the social discursivities that hold out meaning to the subject—just like a word receives meaning from the sentence in which it is embedded.

One more difference between a dichotomising ethics and the Lacanian version is apparent in their respective attitudes to the ego. Sartre stated that "hell is the other" because the other makes a demand on the subject. Lacan argues (Lacan, 1966, session 4) that Sartre's other is actually a mirror image of the ego as it is reflected in the other, as a result of which hell is not really the other but the ego. The ego's field of action is struggle, but the ego cannot be dismantled by means of dispute—dispute only boosts its structure. The way to set oneself free from the ego (by way of an inferno) should not be through resisting the Symbolic order or the social structures, but by using them well. Patients may complain about social norms which seem to get in the way of their pleasure, but once they deepen their work in treatment they find out that the normative demand is nothing but a tool they are using in order to limit their jouissance, a limit that makes their desire possible.

Say a patient complains about his fitness trainer that he's like a tyrant, like what Rousseau called "an oppressive power" who gets in the way of his liberty or pleasure (in this case, the pleasure of being lazy or taking it easy). On being asked, "Who's paying this trainer?" the patient replies, "Me of course". The Symbolic order operates in the service of the subject and it is part of its job to extract the desire for physical activity from him. This trivial insight can be brought to bear at less trivial junctures. When a patient complains about his boss acting like a tyrant, the boss can also be seen as a function that helps to keep jouissance within bounds and support desire. While a patient may view herself as an employee, merely being productive for the organisation's goals, she may in the end come to view the organisation as working for her, to view her boss as "in charge of challenging her" within the organisation that is "her life".

Ethics and esthetics

The ethics of desire assumes that subjects must deal with lack as inalienable part of their experience. In fact, lack which the subject experiences as loss (of earlier or Imaginary objects) really originates in the split nature of language. While it can be experienced as frustrating, as a reason to complain, it can also be felt as desire. One very powerful example of how desire, pleasure and even satisfaction are a function of an experience of lack, is esthetic experience. Esthetic experience pleases the senses not by gratifying needs, but by actually upholding subjects' desire and supporting them to contain lack. The catharsis that occurs at the end of the tragedy is a case in point: the hero does not achieve satisfaction. Release is found in the realisation that the experience of lack is inevitable. This recognition leads to a drop in the tension caused in the always-frustrating belief that full satisfaction is possible.

The neurotic belief in prohibitions and curbs obscures the fact that perfect, enduring satisfaction is impossible. Thus, obsessive personalities will rather relate to pleasure as forbidden than confront the less than complete nature of satisfaction. Hysterical patients, by contrast, tend to approach pleasure as possible though out of reach due to unfairness or discrimination. Beliefs like these keep intact the fantasy of full satisfaction (if only it was allowed or if only things were fair). This fantasy, based in a belief in an Imaginary castrating father, who is forbidding and unjust, is like a story, a plot that makes both yearning and jouissance possible.

While early in treatment patients believe in having been dealt with unfairly ("My parents never allowed me; it wasn't fair"), they eventually come to be aware of the symbolic function, due to which not everything is possible. Because of it everything comes at a price and the father too is subject to these same laws (unlike the Imaginary father who is believed to have special powers). The symbolic function is the function of a law without legislator. A father can position himself either as an Imaginary father, taking on the persona of a tyrant (when, for example, he tells his child, "Now you put on that safety belt because I'm telling you!") or as a father who is equally subject to the symbolic system (when he says: "I have to wear a safety belt too"). Recognition of this principle enables movement from the forbidden to the impossible, from morality to esthetics, from lack as complaint to lack as desire. When the tragedy comes to an end the esthetic effect is in the recognition that it is impossible to escape fate, impossible to gain perfect satisfaction. Having reached this point, the mythological object remains as lost as it was before, but now without guilt and without blame (the hallmarks of neurosis). Catharsis is the result of liberation from the Imaginary father. It comes with a sense that there is no one to blame, that it's simply written that way, in the symbolic-as-system, as a structure (Lacan, 1992 [1959], p. 244).

Sublimation as creativity in the face of lack

Freud defined sublimation as the channelling of sexual energy into an activity resembling a socially acceptable symptom (expressing the yoyeuristic drive in photography, for instance). Unlike Freud who considers the libido as originally linked to a real object then to be transferred to an alternative, symbolic object, Lacan argues that the drive is underwritten by symbolisation, that the body's erogenous zones developed as a result of such symbolisation—in other words: the real object, too, is symbolic from the outset. Lacan moreover argues that the act of symbolisation itself is responsible for libidinal charging. When, by way of expressing fondness, one pinches a child's cheek, one actually isolates the cheek and libidinally charges it as a site of desire (the parent's desire toward the child). This marking gives rise to the boy's urge to kiss his girlfriend's cheek. The cheek is marked as an erotic site, rather than as the result of a transfer of libido from one site on the body to another, because of having been addressed, marked as such.

If a figurative painting constitutes a sublimating displacement of libido, in Freud's terms, from the world onto the canvas—the replacement of the object by a signifier—then an abstract or conceptual painting which represents no reality in this world is a fundamentally novel phenomenon, a new type of signifier. As the abstract painting does not refer to a prior object, the spectators do not identify it and this generates a new discourse. Hence it might be argued that sublimation in the Lacanian sense is not about representing a real object but about a lack, the lack of an earlier signifier, and this is what generates meaning, namely, the resulting discourse.

In the clinic, the analyst will search for esthetic or poetic formulations of the lack the patient's text expresses. Thus, the decision to stop the session (see the subsection "The Short Session", below) is entailed by what one may call esthetic considerations. Closing a circle is one illustration of the poetic effect in treatment. If the patient starts the meeting by announcing, "Sorry I'm late", then to go on talking about the difficulty he has giving up on alternatives and making decisions, the analyst may conclude the meeting saying: "It's hard to give up one thing to be on time for the other." Or, if to begin with the patient spoke about burdens, and at the end forgets her coat, then the analyst may pick up the question of the burden she left in the clinic.

Shedding belief in fullness as a condition for extracting desire from a symptom

And so, lack is inherent to human nature and any ethics, therefore, that hides this lack by means of universality, norms, imperatives or jouissance does not suit psychoanalytic healing. Esthetic, cathartic effects (whether in tragedy or comedy; in the visual arts or in music) rather than being the fruit of gratified desire, are born of the recognition of its impossibility. In the absence of an esthetic mould that lends shape to the absent lack, symptoms persistently maintain it as against the imaginary utopia of fullness—for such fullness leaves no room for desire, or, put differently, for subjective positioning. Hence a psychoanalytic ethics seeks to replace the denial of lack, and the present symptoms, with manifestations of desire.

A typical example of the denial of lack in people with neurosis is guilt. Sometimes guilt offers a way of holding on to an Imaginary Other (as in: "I am guilty, therefore there is someone to be guilty towards").

The implied assumption is that the other has a lack, not we, and we are to blame for not fulfilling that lack. Such guilt belongs in a structure that relieves individuals of responsibility for their desire—and so the treatment aims to undo this structure. Once the various reasons for guilt towards the other have been addressed, the more elusive guilt of subjects *vis-a-vis* themselves comes into view. Here the issue is avoidance of going with their desire. This guilt is obviously valuable for the treatment's progress. Test anxiety, for instance, can be seen as guilt about unsatisfactory learning. Who, however, says what's satisfactory? Any answers that concern others' expectations (teacher, parents) relate to the first type of guilt. From this guilt, however, another guilt, about not acting on one's desire, can be derived (where the time a person devotes to her or his studies is not in tune with their desire). Owning one's desire does not imply that this desire originates exclusively "inside", as many existentialists would have it. Desire necessarily involves the desire of others (e.g., parents and forefathers). Owning one's desire refers to adopting it, it is its subjectivisation. My desire is not free of the desire of others: it is desire which I own as mine (regardless of its sources, given that desire anyhow comes from the other).

The insight that blaming others (even those who never demanded anything) results from blaming ourselves for neglecting our desire is ground for optimism. When an interpretation identifies the desire in blame, this may undo guilt and define desire. The treatment, in this way, may relieve obsessive patients of their chronic ambivalence and allow them to create a better fit between their desire and their action. Ambivalence often renders the impossible wish for pure desire. The subject gets stuck between fulfilling the desires that are aimed at her and remaining without desires of her own—depression occurs when she refuses to desire because it is not purified of the Other. She gives up altogether. The aim is to help the patient choose: this way or that. And to stop her from attributing the reason for her action to others' wishes. As the will is inherently unconscious—among other things because of its illegitimacy—issues concerning the will are not easily clarified. The effect of removing repression in psychoanalysis is a shirking of domination and, at the same time, assuming responsibility over desire.

The question regarding the relations between action and desire is more accurately formulated as follows: "Have you acted in conformity with the desire that is in you?" (Lacan, 1992 [1959], p. 314). This way of putting it takes into account the fact that we do not choose desire, that it rather exists within us as part of us. This doesn't imply that it exists in any *a-priori* form and that all we need to do is discover it. That is the error of the obsessive person who believes that all he needs to do is to first know his desire and then act on it—an error that exposes him to interminable doubt. Desire occurs in the very act, in paying the price, in the effort, and in the willingness to wager on the outcome. To put it differently: there is no wish without act. In order to make a choice that is not neurotic, we must give ourselves account of the fact that we don't choose desire but adopt it, acknowledge it, love it and go with it: we see ourselves as its object, an object in the human-symbolic setup, of generations of subjects who have constituted the language into which we were born, for it is the Other of culture that determines the conditions of desire. Once we acknowledge that the negotiations about the degree in which we invest in desire rather than taking place before others, occur before ourselves, we recognise, also, that assuming responsibility for desire involves the regulation of jouissance, that it and desire are at each other's expense. Freedom, in these terms, is not freedom from an imaginary authority, which we recognise by the presence of guilt, but the freedom to choose to what extent we pay for desire by giving up on jouissance and the other way around. The part of desire that does not express itself in action or in paying a price for it, will take the form of distress, regret or guilt. Distress renders bodily the principle of the excess of jouissance when one refuses to resign it, to pay in jouissance as the price of desire.

The analyst's desire

Lacan believed that the psychoanalyst's desire plays a crucial role in how the treatment proceeds (Lacan, 2002 [1958a]). If desire constitutes reality, then the psychoanalytic reality is constituted by the psychoanalyst's desire. That desire, in turn, is supported by the ethics that propels him, the values he goes by. What distinguishes the psychoanalytic structure of desire from the neurotic structure of desire? In the case of analysts, too, it is lack that instigates desire. While the person who is the analyst is not exempted from having a clinical structure of her own, the desire of this person insofar as he is an analyst is a particular instance of desire, applied in a singular way. The very basis of psychoanalytic desire is formed by no longer believing in the Imaginary Other, the neurotic assumption that perfection is possible. At the end of psychoanalysis, the analysand accepts that there is no one who ordains that we give up jouissance. This realisation helps the analyst not to fall into the patient's trap—namely, to take on the role of the Other. When the patient asks: "Should I stop drinking and driving?" the analyst may be tempted to position herself as the Other and to reply emphatically, "You most certainly should!" Having recognised that there is no Other helps the analyst to take a different position, one that indicates the patient's lack (by suggesting, for instance, the hard time the patient is having with the loss of his authoritarian father, or his difficulty making up his own mind).

There is a hysterical side to the analyst's desire because it is his aim to arouse the patient's desire. Typically, this hysterical structure, to pro- tract yearning, bars both himself and the patient from being gratified. The analyst listens and waits for more to be said, and he stimulates free association. The hysterical person does not know that he wants to arouse desire. He believes he wants to be the object of desire: hence when he arouses the other's desire and it is not directed at him, he is narcissisti- cally injured. The analyst, by contrast, has to agree to arouse the patient's desire but not in order to be the object of that desire. When the analysis comes to an end the analyst faces that he is not the object of the patient's desire, and he must be ready to accept this from the start.

The obsessive personality structure typically refuses to surrender the utopia of eternity. This refusal makes it hard for such individuals to yearn as the imaginary utopia is based on the refusal to acknowl- edge object loss (so that if it was never lost, then how can one yearn for it?). Hypochondria, for instance, the obsessive fear of dying as the result of disease, keeps intact a doubt regarding the very necessity of death—otherwise put: it maintains the illusion that it's possible not to die. The analyst's position must take death into account, which means that she impedes the obsessive doubt. The analyst's own conviction regarding object loss is obviously usually the result of having under- gone psychoanalysis herself, as a condition for taking her own position as a psychoanalyst.

The analyst's desire, then, does not envision harmony, the elimination of all conflict, or the establishment of a loved and desirable self. Lacan criticises ego psychology's notion that the analyst should take an ideal position and serve as an object of identification for the patient thus to enable the latter to construct her or his personality on these lines (Lacan calls this type of identification with the analyst getting "swallowed", a type of cannibalism). Recognition of the lack of the Other, reached at termination, will also involve the recognition that harmony or fusion are impossible (and that lack always remains). This insight also contradicts blind obedience to and respect for authority, including the identification of the analyst with authority. Even if the latter positions herself as one who is supposed to know, she doesn't really believe in this. This absence of one who is supposed to know, and the subsequent collapse of identifications, decrees a certain orphanhood, and this creates a desire for absolute difference rather than similarity—that is: identification. Comparisons are fundamentally narcissistic—they refer to reflections, to the image. When identifications topple, we can no longer go on believing that knowing what the neighbour does will help us know better what we want ourselves.

Another absolute difference sought by the analyst is the one between past and future (Lacan, 2002 [1964b]). There is a certain repetitive drive to reproduce a first, lost pleasure. As it will never be possible to repeat this experience, any attempt at achieving it is doomed. This is why the analyst's support of desire is associated with a focus on innovation, difference, the element of surprise in the patient's complaint of repetitiveness. A married patient who fell in love with another man and feared for her marriage, came to recognise, in treatment, the identificatory character of her infatuation. It was through the man she fell in love with that she actually came closer to herself—they laughed together, allowing her to find out that she was funny—with her husband she did not laugh. Affirmation of her desire for laughter helped her rid herself of the infatuation which enveloped this desire. Lacanian oriented treatment enables subjects to recognise their singularity—not as a result of some extraneous validation but as a function of their very yearning.

Originality and surprise take the place of the lost illusion that the object can be restored. Therefore, the analyst's desire is also a desire to dismantle the patient's perception of reality which, in its solidness, generates superfluous suffering—and he does this among other things by means of pointing attention to surprises that turn up in the patient's text, offering an opportunity for something new to develop. The subversive component of rupture aims to illustrate the fact that reality is a creation. The analyst takes on the role of an editor who punctuates and interprets the patient's words, on the assumption that the artist is the patient's unconscious. This process of editing comes to make public, or publish, desire. The analyst must avoid positioning her or himself as a creator in order not to be the one who invents or creates the patient's reality on the latter's behalf.

A patient, for instance, recognised that his own depression included an element of identification with his father's depression. Separating from the depression thus is bound to result in leaving the father with his own depression, and himself robbed of a model of identification, without a partner, without a source (reproduction of the father's depression constitutes depression by way of an origin). Once there is recognition of the fact that no authority actually determines how he is to feel, and that there is no one to identify with, he feels free and intimidated at the same time. As the ground collapsed under his feet, he asked: "So now what?" He had always drawn on his father as an example. When this question comes up, the analyst should avoid giving the patient any directions thereby offering himself as a new authority taking the place of the father. This avoidance opens an opportunity for invention.

Escaping repetition can also be described as a weakening of the death instinct, which can be viewed as pursuit of the lost object for the sake of full satisfaction—or what Freud called nirvana in *Beyond the Pleasure Principle*. The life instinct, by contrast, accepts lack. Hence even an analyst's too close adherence to theory may become an object of nirvana.

The analyst's position without reference to the patient

If we, as analysts had to know only one thing about positioning ourselves prior to the encounter with the patient, our choice may well be: "We need nothing from the patient." One implication of Lacan's structural approach—according to which desire is determined by symbolic-structural elements—is that the therapeutic setting, itself, is a structure. This structure has two foci: the wanted object and the wanting subject. As the analyst positions herself as object, the patient is forced to take a subject position. Lacan considers intersubjective approaches, which orient themselves toward a subject-subject relationship, as an epitome of imaginary relations with the mirror image.

As she (almost ascetically) abstains from wanting anything from her patient, the analyst leaves the burden of the will to the patient. The neurotic patient will try not to have to carry this burden and tempt the analyst to want on his behalf. The above-mentioned stance "We need nothing from the patient" will frustrate the patient and make him demanding. It is this demandingness that will enable the analyst then to interpret and to extract his desire. Wherever the analyst slips and nevertheless expresses something she needs from the patient—even if this concerns her wish for the patient to become well—she actually relieves him of the burden of the will which constitutes him as a subject. Even analysts who do believe it is their task to want something of their patients may—because of being troubled by their own personal issues, for instance—find at some junctures that when leaving their patients to their own devices, with their own wishes, some unforeseen therapeutic effects actually occur.

This is not to say that analysts don't experience desire, but that they do not yearn for the object, which is located on the side of their patients. Even as desire constitutes the subject, the desire of psychoanalysts—which involves not wanting anything from their patients—constitutes them as analysts. Their object of desire is the uncovering of the unconscious and its interpretation. By taking the position of not needing anything from their neurotic patients they undermine the latter's script in which the analyst is someone who makes demands (this is more obvious in the case of obsessive patients than of hysteric patients) about learning how to refrain from jouissance or to stick to the norms, for instance. This leaves patients unsure: they are used to using the other's will as a coordinate of their own. Either they please the other or they revolt against her.

The clinic, of course, abounds with compromise, and no analyst is wholly free of wanting something from patients. Thus, Lacan considers patients' acting out as reactions to their analyst's desire (originating in normative prejudice, or in a patient's manipulation aimed to drag the analyst into a demanding role)—he attributes it, in other words, to analysts' failure, to a crossing of boundaries. Once the failure is spotted and interpreted, the treatment is back on track (Lacan, 2002 [1958a], pp. 500–501). The patient's demand can take a plethora of shapes—explicit and implicit: "Can't you give me a reduction?", "Let's set a different time", "So what do you think is the right thing to do in such a case?", "What do you recommend I should read if I want to know about Lacan?" Meeting such demands will lead to further demands. This characteristic of demands distinguishes them from requests that are not demands. Demands, being attempts at formulating desire and not to be satisfied, will go on until they are frustrated. So, for instance, when a patient asks to change the time of a meeting this in itself is not necessarily a demand—but if she goes on apologising about it, she constructs a logical constellation in which the analyst features as the demanding, unsatisfied Other.

For Lacan God's act of preventing Abraham to sacrifice Isaac is an illustration of the collapse of the demanding Other. From then on it becomes impossible to attribute to God demands that must be fulfilled, and to evade yearning. In the story of Isaac's binding, the victim is not Isaac, whose sacrifice underwrites the logical structure of the Other, but rather God himself, the demanding Other, the idol. Abraham is required to sacrifice the idea of someone for whom sacrifices must be made (Julien, 1995, p. 106). In his book *On the Names of the Father* (Lacan, 2013), Lacan quotes the medieval rabbinical authority Rashi, who has Abraham asking God if he may leave at least a little scratch, draw some blood, so he may please God, and in fact stick to God in his role of the demanding divinity. In contrast with one who uses words like "must", "has to", and "no choice" which all point at an Other who is the source of all obligations, the analyst takes a sceptical position. This scepticism does not only challenge the patient to think in terms of free choice, but also exposes the fantasy that includes the demanding Other, with all its associated desire and jouissance. From the demand—attributed to God—for Abraham's offspring in the story of Isaac's binding, one may derive Abraham's desire for offspring—a desire that takes the form of God's promise to Abraham that his seed will multiply like the stars in heaven and like the sand on the shore. Struggling with the fact that no demand is directed at him, Abraham opens his eyes to the fact that there is no imaginary idol who demands his son, and to the existence of a symbolic God who interprets his wish for offspring as plenteous as the sand on the sea shore. Thus, the frustration of the demand enables the formulation of desire.

At work in the clinic, the demand must of course be frustrated within the limits of the transference. The more powerful and positive the transference, the better able the patient will be to tolerate frustration without dropping out of treatment. The analyst must regulate the degree to which she declines the role of the Other in accordance to the patient's ability to take this as part of the treatment. Moving to the couch illustrates how transference relations can be exploited to reduce the position of the demanding Other. When they meet face to face, the patient adjusts herself to the psychoanalyst's wishes insofar as she deduces them from the psychoanalyst's facial expressions. When the latter looks bored, she will change subject, and she will develop the subject when the psychoanalyst shows interest. Moving to the couch robs the patient of these cues and undermines her reliance on the imaginary expectations (demands) she attributes to the psychoanalyst-Other. Thus, there are patients who refuse to lie on the couch and give up on the eye contact that supports the Imaginary aspect of the transference. The suggestion to move to the couch assumes a strong enough transference relationship for the patient to be able to omit the Other's demand as a compass guiding her desire. Moving to the couch does not diminish the Imaginary aspect of the Other's demand but it does show us that the Other's demand is a fantasy of the subject.

Generally speaking, while in psychotherapy therapists take the position of authority in the sense that they help to give meaning, Lacanian psychoanalysis looks to shape the treatment as a symbolic space for the interpretation of patients' text—here analysts don't serve as demanding Imaginary Others or as authorities who bestow meaning on what patients say. Giving meaning may often help alleviate the symptom with which patients came into psychotherapy, and there are patients who will feel that this is enough for them. Others, their curiosity whetted by the encounter with their unconscious, will continue in psychoanalysis. We may argue that a successful treatment will have proved the existence of the unconscious and will have aroused a desire or transference strong enough to cope with the un-understood that marks psychoanalysis (and which it sees as valuable for the earlier mentioned reasons, namely that it stimulates creativity and inventiveness). Psychoanalysis attenuates the need for answers, and in that sense one might say that it trains every analysand to become an analyst. Getting answers regarding patients' own lives, after all, doesn't necessarily put them in the position to give answers to other patients—the ability to face the absence of an answer, however, is something that can be passed on.

CHAPTER TWO

The clinic as a symbolic space

T
he analytic space is a kind of theatre composed of symbols. The more defined and consistent the set, the more unlike other spaces in his life, the easier it will be for the patient to get immersed in the treatment, to familiarise himself with its "local culture" and move into free associations which, in their turn, are part of the symbolic-ritual process of analytical psychotherapy. Time, money, the way the clinic is furnished, the analyst's typical intonation, contracts and agreements (regarding cancellations, for instance), how the patient enters the clinic, how they shake hands, how he moves toward the couch—these are what make up this process. So powerful is the reality of this Symbolic domain that a patient may fail to recognise his analyst outside the Symbolic domain of the clinic.

The analyst uses the symbolic setting of the clinic in order to advance healing according to the theoretical principles that guide him. These principles manifest themselves in each and every response to a phone call, to every practical reference to time, money, cancellations, late arrivals, referrals, gifts, and the other pieces of the symbolic puzzle that constitutes the clinic. Obviously, analysts may share theoretical principles yet reach totally different practical conclusions. And so, the practical issues discussed in this chapter are only meaningful in the

29

context of the theoretical insight that underlies them, and they should therefore be regarded as nothing more than illustrations of a praxis that is based on a theory.

The first telephone conversation, payment, cancellations and late arrivals, making notes, and eye contact

The first telephone conversation

Usually the first contact between patient and analyst is via the telephone. It is a good idea to already use this opportunity to establish the patient as a desiring subject, by for instance asking questions like: "When would you like to meet?" and "Why do you seek treatment?" In this conversation moreover, the patient is likely to ask how much a session will cost. One may respond that payment is something that can be discussed on meeting as it depends, among other things, on the patient's means.

Payment

Money plays a critical symbolic role because payment is a constant reminder that the analyst is neither parent nor friend. If the patient brings into the therapeutic relationship social, romantic or familial expectations, it may be better to require payment after each session. Formalists expect all their patients to pay at the end of each session. This also prevents obsessive patients from running up bills in order then to position themselves as compulsive debtors (and the analyst as a claimant), and keeps hysterical patients from positioning themselves as badly done by (it is of course worth not to miss the opportunity to interpret the patient's unconscious desire to be wanted or demanded, or to be loved and special, depending on what stage in the transference relations the treatment has reached).

Questions of payment are part of the analyst's freedom. So as not to fall victim to his own neuroses, it is advisable for the analyst to be free of concerns regarding payment and senses of exploitation or bitterness regarding the patient. It is moreover best for the analyst to be free to speak or to be silent as he wishes, or to terminate a session as he sees fit (this is elaborated below). The less preoccupied the analyst is by issues concerning payment or time management the better able will he be to abandon his position as subject, who experiences lack and desire, in order to surrender this place to the patient.

Cancellations and late arrivals

Cancellations and changes in appointment times are crucially signifi-cant in treatment, both by offering material for interpretation and in so far as they affect the analytic space—which must be protected for the sake of the analyst's freedom and the patient's commitment. The com-mon rule is that cancellations or changes in times must be announced at least twenty-four hours ahead, otherwise the patient will be charged. If a patient time and again cancels twenty-five hours in advance, the rule might be changed and the patient could be charged for a meeting as soon as he makes the appointment. Interpretation, here too, is advis-able (and in accordance with other relevant indications relating to the treatment: "You want to figure out to what extent people are ready to put up with you and to accept the damage you cause"; "You want to be given a clear boundary to protect you against your own impulses").

In case of a misunderstanding about the time of the meeting, there's no fundamental reason not to be lenient, once or twice, on the assump-tion that if this is not a matter of a symptom then it will surely not hap-pen again. But where there are repeated cancellations or late arrivals, the analyst's leniency will cause the symptom to worsen. Recurrent cancellations can be used to convey an ethical message about the differ-ence between guilt and responsibility. If a patient expresses guilt toward the analyst for having cancelled a meeting, one may suggest he pay for the missed meeting in order to put an end to the guilt of which he com-plains. If a patient expresses reluctance to pay for a meeting one may interpret: "You rather pay me with the pain of guilt than with money?"; "Is guilt really cheaper?"; "Do you tend generally to stay guilty rather than taking responsibility for reparation?"; "By paying me in suffering, you seem to assume that people enjoy your suffering as if it was a sort of alternative payment—do you think of one who asks for money as a sadist?" and so on.

Late arrivals, too, may be significant, though not with a fit-for-all meaning. If a generic interpretation, nevertheless, is made, it tells more about the analyst's symptom (interpreting every late coming as disre-spectful, for instance, may disclose the analyst's symptomatic position-ing of himself as one who tends to be taken lightly). Lateness may be taken to express aggressiveness; avoiding a sense of emptiness or avoiding having to spend time in the waiting room because it is experienced as a humiliation; a request for signs of caring, or a challenge of the clock which represents death; lateness may also say something about the jouissance of the symptom ("I couldn't give up on just one more game on the computer"; "I drive like a madman when I'm late"). There's an infinity of possible interpretations, and it is therefore important each time anew to check. A patient, for instance, who spent time in jail, is late in getting to the bus stop on his way to work, every morning; he then chases the bus and sometimes misses it. When asked how he felt when he caught the bus in time, he replied: "I was glad I managed to catch the bus, that I didn't throw away another working day." Here the interpretation may well be that he takes risks in order to feel that he "manages"—given his sense of having missed out on things while being in jail. Late arrival may thus be regarded as a form of acting out which deserves to be interpreted, both so it does not grow worse and in order to release the desire and the jouissance which it helps to maintain. As a rule, if the interpretation does not affect the lateness, it's best to look for other meanings.

Making notes

If the analyst makes notes in the course of the face-to-face session the patient may feel that he is not being heard. This then is likely to draw him out of the subject position, while it is the main objective of the treatment for him to take that position. If the patient lies on the couch, however, the analyst should write down what he says, not by way of recording but in order to read the patient's speech as though it were a text, even as he is speaking. This reading of the patient's words as text is one of the key ways of relating to the subject of the unconscious, the hypothetical entity behind his unconscious motives. It is more natural to hear things in terms of conscious conventions when listening to speech. Manifesting themselves in the patient's tone and his conscious emphases, his conscious intentions will interfere with the analyst's ability to read the text itself. Reading affords a better way into the unconscious connections in the patient's speech. Much like there is a difference between listening to a poet reading from his writings and reading the same poems oneself, listening-reading in relation to the patient's text without attending to his voice and persona exposes meanings of which the speaker himself was unaware. This type of listening-reading does not replace Freud's notion of evenly hovering attention. "Reading" too must hover and not look for anything specific in such a way that connections will reveal themselves.

To illustrate, a patient who tends to be rejected by men mentioned going to the supermarket. The man she admires and is interested in said that "a super woman is almost a man". Bringing together these two statements serves as a basis for the interpretation: "A super-man will give you market value."

It is easier, moreover, to identify combinations of letters, motifs, or recurrent expressions when reading as the ear is used to ignore them. If a patient, for instance, frequently repeats "I don't have" in diverse forms ("I don't have money today", "I don't have anything to say") it will be easier to pick up on the link between these statements and to ask: "What is it that you don't have?", while the question in the background is: "What desire can spring from the lack that is present in the statement 'I don't have'?"

There is a fundamental difference between relating to the patient's text and to his body language, tics, changes in dress or hairstyle, which tends to position the patient as object and therefore is best avoided (even where the patient will be disappointed because we have failed to refer to his weight loss, for instance). Attention to words, by contrast, consti-tutes the patient as subject by remarking on the interconnections occur-ring in his text. Thus, when the same word appeared in an ostensibly different context, pointing out this context is tantamount to pointing out the unconscious in action—or rather: the subject of the unconscious (the unconscious function of choice). As a result, the patient identifies less with the socially recognised figure and more with this mysterious unconscious factor that guides his choices, directs the text, and makes the connections between his words that emerged through interpretation.

First sessions

No initial interview is held in Lacanian treatment, nor is there any struc-tured examination of the patient's mental status. Instead the patient is allowed to freely say what he wants, with minimum interference, right from the first meeting. A general prompt can be something like this ques-tion: "What brings you here?"; "What hurts?"; "What is it you want?"; "How can I help?" and information (about the patient's childhood, earlier therapies, etc.) can be gathered as the free speech goes on. Still, the first session has some typical specific functions. It is recommended that the patient articulate a complaint or wish that made him come for treatment.

Statements like "It's mandatory if you want to study psychology", or "My wife told me to come", do not convey the patient's wish. "I don't want to lose my wife", by contrast, does. The first session also offers an experience of analytic work, among other things because it proposes a different perspective for thinking about things, even if it concerns only a minor issue. Such a fresh perspective helps in establishing the transference. The first meeting is generally too soon to point out his own responsibility for his anguish to the patient: since he doesn't yet understand the actions of the unconscious he cannot distinguish between guilt and responsibility. Still, a different angle on the facts can give hope for change.

How does one invite free association? Since repression exercises its censorship, unpaved roads have to be taken and hence it is important to tell the patient to say anything that comes to mind, without criticism and without filtering. There is an advantage, moreover, to letting the session evolve without any prior agenda: it leaves space for surprise, for breaching obstacles and for bypassing repression. If it is the patient's task to say anything that comes to mind at a given moment, it is the analyst's role to collect expressions of the unconscious: errors, slips of the tongue, recurrent motifs, jokes or parallels, and by means of them to point out unconscious desires. The relations between conscious and unconscious resemble those of a game of odds-and-evens between an adult and a child. Again and again the adult wins because he understands the child's pattern. When the child understands that the adult reads his thoughts and anticipates his choices he can do nothing to reverse the situation because the adult will also know about that. The unconscious can be compared to an adult who sees the whole picture, and the conscious, here, can be likened to a child. The child may win at least part of the time if he doesn't try to think and makes his choices by throwing a coin. In that case the adult won't be able to predict the child's actions. Speech in conditions of free association is like throwing a coin: it opens a possibility for new interpretation by skirting unconscious censorship.

Ego and imaginary identification in the early stages of treatment

In the early stages of treatment, in the work with neurotic patients as well, room must be given to the ego by means of the analyst's willingness to be the object of admiration or idealisation, to be attributed magical, omnipotent knowledge—knowledge, in other words, that exceeds the professional ("You probably know what this dream means"; "I'm sure you know what I'm going to say"). This attribution of knowledge plays an important role in creating the foundations of the transference relations. The analyst, of course, should take care not to assume that he actually is in possession of such knowledge, that is, to fall into the trap of imaginary identification with his own ego.

As mentioned in the previous chapter, Lacan invented a myth describing the emergence of the ego, which he called the "mirror stage". The young child who looks into the mirror erroneously concludes that he and his image are one and the same thing. He wants to believe this because this identity allows him to perceive himself as a clear-cut, integrated figure with an outline that covers up for his fragmentary experience. Turning to his parents, who are a great Other, representatives of the Symbolic order, with the question "Is that me?" they answer him by supporting his imaginary identity: "Yes, that's you!" (Lacan, J., 2002 [1958b], pp. 77–78). One can recognise a repetition of the mirror stage in the idealising relations with the analyst. The patient assumes that the analyst sees him as an integral figure and has the ability to define him and tell him who he is (at times, this appears as an explicit request: "Tell me if I'm normal!"). This assumption maintains the patient as an ego in the analyst's perception. The ego grows weaker in the course of the treatment and its place is taken by the subject. While the former evolves on the basis of the body's image in the mirror, the latter is a product of language. The subject is the unconsciously desiring one who is revealed through the desire made manifest by his words or actions. This is why the subject is considered the agent of Freudian slips, exactly what shatters the ego-figure's unity.

Ambiguity, as said, assists in this transition from belief in the ego's unity to the emergence of the subject. From the perspective of the ego, ambiguity appears as ignorance or imperfection because it contradicts the myth of unity, of one meaning. As the treatment progresses it becomes clear that there is no correct meaning, that lack of clarity is inherent and that from the plurality of clashing meanings follows the emergence of the subject who will decide between them by taking a position (or the subject of the unconscious who exists given the fact that the position was already taken in the unconscious).

Analytic listening and encouraging speech and desire

Freud introduced the notion of "evenly suspended attention" or "hovering attention", which refers to the analyst refraining from attending to any specific meaning in the patient's words (Freud, 1912e). Such listening acts like a net, ready to capture something when it comes but without knowing what. The analyst attends in order to be surprised. Even if his net doesn't catch anything through an entire meeting, it's important the analyst doesn't force himself to speak. Quiet listening without intervention is extremely valuable. Moments of silence may occur which will be broken by the patient saying something he didn't dare to say until then. This is why it is sometimes necessary to maintain a position of non-response to the patient's expectations for dialogue and his demand to be released from his anguish for the sake of the treatment's progress. Anguish is the price to be paid if one wishes to open the unconscious and overcome repressions.

In addition to the above, the analyst's attention is fuelled by two key objectives: desire and jouissance. These are embodied in, among other things, the classic "suspects" of the analyst's listening: Freudian slips or parapraxes, failures in action, relationships that display unconscious oedipal relations, as well as repetitions in form or subject matter. Desire takes many shapes, from casual mentions of appetite to various modes of feeling, demand, expectation and deprivation. Jouissance, excitement beyond pleasure, has different manifestations too, including pain, shock, and aversion.

In everyday listening our point of departure is that we are understood and that we in turn understand our interlocutors. In analytic psychotherapy we start with the opposite assumption. When the patient tells us about an experience that seems familiar to us we must not take it for granted that we understand either its causes or its nature. A woman patient of over eighty years old, for instance, before undergoing surgery talked about her fear of dying. In a conversation an unexpected reason for her fear emerged: there was a secret she worried she was going to have to carry into her grave. The criterion for irregularities in a patient's text that are worth consideration is not normalcy as the analyst thinks of it, but the text's internal consistency. If the patient talks about someone angrily and the next time with guilt, it's fitting to give pause. The point here is not to urge the patient to make up his mind or to expose his lie but to face him with the contradiction in order to consider its nature. He may feel guilty, for instance, at the very fact of being angry for having to fulfil some unfeasible, nearly self-sacrificing ideal of kind heartedness. In the end, then, reflection on the contradiction evolves into reflection on the patient's belief in any kind of ideal of which he isn't really sure what he thinks.

Another form of inconsistency is when the narrative flow of the patient's account is broken. Dropped parts may point at repression, as do statements of the kind: "No matter, that's of no consequence", whether they occur in the context of missing details or in relation to something the patient himself said. Another way of distancing what is being said which might point in the direction of repression is when a person changes either his accent or his language in mid-speech.

Another form of Lacanian listening is by privileging signifier over signified—a preference for surface listening over deep listening. The assumption is that the repressed rather than being buried somewhere deep down is there for all to see. But when it appears in a different context, in a different semantic context, one might very easily fail to see it. It's like when a librarian is trying to hide a book in the library by hiding its filing card while the book is simply on the shelf. A patient told me her car was towed away from a spot at which there was a clear sign announcing that cars would be towed away. She said: "What a misfortune." Thinking through the prism of "deep meaning" one might have concluded she was irresponsible, or that this was a provocation intended to manoeuvre the analyst into the role of educator. But stress on the word *fortune* triggered associations. *Fortune* was the name of an aunt who had been like a mother to her. Remembering this aunt brought tears to her eyes. The signifier "miss-*Fortune*" expressed a sense of being orphaned. Another patient told about an error she had made "inadvertently" (in Hebrew *tom-lev*). Her mistake was to have authorised payment of something that went to a boy suffering from a developmental disability, against the instructions of the organisation for which she worked. The analyst reminded her that her own brother, who suffered from a developmental disability, was called Tom. *Fortune* and *Tom*, in these cases, were spoken as words (rather than names) and had they been analysed for their semantic meaning their emotional charge would not have been picked up. That is to say, it wasn't the names that were repressed: only their context was, like in the case of the filing cards in the library.

Even when a patient uses a common expression which does not seem to invite identification of personal meanings, the analyst is free to look for them. When a young patient says, "a real son of a bitch" (slang for something very good), the analyst may suggest to him that this is a violent or sexual expression. Though the patient may dismiss the analyst as anachronistic, subsequent associations will confirm or disprove the interpretation. Confirmation for an interpretation is not usually or necessarily forthcoming right away. Optimal confirmation derives from the unconscious, in the shape of a string of associations, recollection of a dream or physical phenomena like anguish (anxiety), a blush or a rise in body temperature.

The main objective of the analyst's questions, like his listening, is to allow the patient to continue talking. Closed questions do not offer an opening for speech and associations. It does not matter, in any case, if he answers the question; in some sense, it's better if he answers the question he thinks he was asked, because this gives us a better notion of what preoccupies him (Fink, 2007, p. 27). The analyst's merest reiteration, with or without a change in intonation, may be enough to bring on more associations. The movement of the signifiers in an association opens consciousness, sets desire into motion, facilitates its flow, and is therefore a goal in its own right. This is also why the analyst should stay close to the patient's language, even if it isn't usually his (i.e., the analyst's).

Since it is the aim of the analysis to discriminate between the desiring subject and the other, the analyst must be alert to elements of suggestibility. Complex questions are likely to work suggestively, and the same is the case, in fact, for any addition of subject matter. Remarks like "You look tired", or "Does this arouse sexual feelings?" may inadvertently plant seeds of tiredness or sexuality in the patient's consciousness, as if they had been present before the remark. A typical illustration of suggestion is the mother's interpretation-statement of her child's wishes. If the child cries and the mother feeds him, she interprets him and thereby constitutes him as already hungry.

Interpretation

In the early years of psychoanalysis Freud found that interpretations explaining the oedipal origins of symptoms removed the symptoms. This was a momentous discovery; patients suffering from paralysis got up and walked. But the potency of interpretation diminished over time (Lacan, 1988 [1954], pp. 10–11). Lacan explains that oedipal interpretation's initial freshness and unusualness were the source of its power. In time Freud's notions concerning the Oedipus complex became a common cultural good, and hence the interpretation grew banal. Though, his work does rely on oedipal interpretation, Lacan stresses that interpretation should be innovative and surprising in order to be effective. The more unexpected the angle from which things are approached, the more successful the interpretation will be in releasing desire from the symptom.

Lacan, as said, considers it an important part of the analyst's role to edit the patient's text—as editing subserves interpretation (Lacan, 2002 [1953], pp. 209–210). Editing, through paying attention to punctuation and emphasis in the text, forms a minimal level of elementary interpretation; it may include repetition of parts of words, trying to supply the endings of unfinished sentences and inserting coughs into the text. Such interventions take a part in determining the meaning of what is being said.

Biographical and structural interpretation

Freud found the roots of neurosis in the patient's biography; childhood events produce inner conflict which then expresses itself in symptoms. While adopting this approach, Lacan also goes beyond it. Symptoms, for him, constitute a symbolic structuring of the desire and jouissance in the patient's present reality. Hence interpretation might either be biographical or structural. As long as the patient is not ready to assume responsibility for his desires, interpretation will tend to be biographical, more external, that is. As treatment progresses, the analyst will increasingly address the patient as responsible for his choices and he will enquire into how the latter uses the symptom for the sake of desire and jouissance. Obviously, these two modes of interpretation are often tightly interwoven. Often jouissance is prompted by biographical causes. Still, though we may agree that a certain symptom evolved under the influence of external factors, the question of why it continues remains unsolved. Emphasis in the structural approach is not on tracing the symptom back in time in order then to resolve it, but on identifying how it profits the patient, that is: how does the symptom maintain his desire and jouissance?

In the case of inhibitions, for instance, plain logic suggests that the child's formative environment put a brake on his drives causing him to have become an inhibited adult, but one might paradoxically say that these inhibitions are the patient's way of deriving jouissance from prohibition. Anal-retentive auto-erotic jouissance in relation to the law undergoes displacement, and desire is maintained by means of the inhibition which turns gratification into an impossibility. Unconscious logic, here, acts like a proposition: "What I pursue cannot be realised and so I can count on it that my jouissance with this desire will not be destroyed by gratification."

This is why an interpretation that seems aimed to get rid of the patient's symptom will lead to anguish due to apprehensions about losing both the desire and the symptom. Similarly, getting rid of symptoms by means of external conditions that stop the symptom (like artificial feeding in the case of anorexia or closing the casino to the gambler) is likely to lead to depression, to the loss, that is of desire and jouissance. Interpretation, therefore, must be directed to the desire and jouissance enfolded in the symptom and not to the symptom's existence as such. Then it will be possible to hold on to the desire and the jouissance of the symptom without recourse to the suffering (Lacan, 1974, session 2). But this is inexact because the symptom is a way of constructing desire, and desire does not exist without symptomatic structuring. Hence Lacan coined the notion of the *sinthome* which describes what is left of the structuring symptom which holds desire and jouissance, but having shed superfluous suffering.

Interpretation and truth

Unicorns have one horn; the statement to the effect that they have two horns is false. The system ruled by the truth-falsehood dichotomy does not take into account that the unicorn simply doesn't exist. The same is true for words: a word doesn't represent something actual in the world. Rather it generates meaning and its truth is measured in relation to the inner consistency of *a priori* definitions. The unicorn is pre-defined as having one horn only, and truth is what agrees with a definition, not with a "thing". This is why Lacan's attitude to truth is as to a "fixed" game and as always partial.

It is by this logic that the Lacanian clinic is ordained to approach absolute truths with caution. A good interpretation is not considered (as Freud sometimes did) one that hits upon the truth, unveils a fact, but one that produces the effect of truth. This is the effect of a formulation that leads to relief from anguish. An opposite illustration of this is when one finds words to describe a traumatic experience—by definition an experience that cannot be put into words. Formulation by other symbolic means—for instance through art—can also have this effect. This very formulation, occurring as one talks to a listening person, has—from the psychother-apeutic perspective—an effect over and beyond removing repression. Even in the absence of an interpretation that decodes repressed materi-als, the fact that things have been formulated and received a response from outside, validates them as a statement. It is therefore not only the analytic psychoanalyst's role to enable the patient's words to be mean-ingful, but also to be their addressee and thus to transform them into a declaration. By affirming the patient realises himself as a subject, as someone who determines who he is through speech. To return to the unicorn who has one horn, if we don't consider truth positivistically as actual fact but as internal consistency, then the analyst's interpreta-tion can be seen as pointing out not facts but the patient's own uncon-scious interpretation. For instance, an interpretation like: "One can tell from your response that you interpreted my lateness as contemptuous", points at the patient's meaning rather than offering new meaning. The analyst's interpretation turns to the patient as subject of an unconscious that interprets and gives meaning. For instance, an adult female patient brought along drawings she made as a child and asked whether they showed the distress she experienced at the time. Rather than: "One can see from the drawings that you suffered", the interpretation was: "One can see from the drawings that you were trying to tell about your suffering"—the drawings reveal her effort to express something, to com-municate her distress. What was identified in the drawings—as in all of the patient's expressions—rather than objective facts, was the existence of a subject trying to bring herself into existence through articulation.

The object of interpretation is always symbolic. The patient's dress style, thus, is not relevant from the interpretive perspective, assuming that interpretation is based on the patient's speech. When a patient, who is talking about a sense of being oppressed, wears a shirt carrying the word "freedom", then one can relate to his way of dressing as a mode of speech because he chose to wear a shirt with this print—but this case is an exception. Interpretations of behaviours, like weight increase or loss, that are not necessarily symbolic may play into the hands of people with neuroses by allowing them not to speak, that is: releasing them of the burden of subjecthood (e.g., where it concerns matters of weight: "If they understand about me without my having to speak up, then there's no need for me to speak"). Such interpretations are differently superfluous in the case of psychotic patients whose status as subject is fragile. They may produce a feeling of persecution, a sense of not being respected as a subject and of being treated, instead, as an object. As mentioned in earlier chapters, a good interpretation is one that puts emphasis on ambiguity and requires the patient as subject to make up his mind. An ambiguous interpretation constitutes the patient as the one who is responsible for the interpretation he chooses. Accepting the lack of perfection inherent in the absence of one correct interpretation is tantamount to letting go of the fantasy of absolute jouissance. Anyhow, since it is in the nature of the signifying system never to reach closure, interpretations and speech will never fully be exhausted. Acceptance of this fact forms the completion of the analysis.

Dream interpretation

According to Freud, and to Lacan after him, a dream always represents a wish. But how and by means of whom does the dream represent a wish?

> "One day I had been explaining to her that dreams are fulfilments of wishes. Next day she brought me a dream in which she was travelling down with her mother-in-law to the place in the country where they were to spend their holidays together. Now I knew that she violently rebelled against the idea of spending the summer near her mother-in-law … Now her dream had undone the solution she had wished for: was this not the sharpest possible contradiction of my theory … The dream showed that I was wrong. Thus, it was her wish that I might be wrong and her dream showed this wish fulfilled" (Freud, 1900a, pp. 151–152).

Freud brings this anecdote to demonstrate how a dream represents the wish as fulfilled if we are focused enough to recognise what the wish is. Freud recognises that the wish is the hysterical wish to object to Freud and prove him wrong. Lacan interpreted it as the hysterical desire to reveal the lack in the Other who is in the role of the master.

The subject of the wish, therefore, is not the main actor of the dream, the ego that is, the protagonist of the dream who suffers the presence of the mother-in-law, but rather the screenwriter whose desire is responsible for concocting the dream, the identity of the one trying to prove Freud wrong. And so, when interpreting the dream, we shall look for the desire of the subject in the desire of the dream's screenwriter, on the assumption that the very existence of the dream is already the fulfilment of a wish. The writer is willing to sacrifice the main actor (to make her suffer in the presence of her mother in law) in order to fulfil the wish (to prove Freud wrong). When a person dreams that his wallet was lost and that his attempts to find it resulted in failure we will assume that his wish was to be rid of his wallet. In free association, we shall look for the desire that this wish embodies: Avoid superiority and conflict? A hysterical desire to maintain desire by means of lack? A patient dreamt he rescued his fellow students at the college which was going up in flames. One could assume that the desire, the wish in this dream, is the heroism of rescuing cherished friends, but this is likely to be the ego's desire, the desire of the dreamer as the protagonist of the dream. If we follow the rule that the subject's desire is the desire of the dream's scriptwriter, we shall ask the patient and ourselves: Why does he want the college to burn down? What fulfilled desire does the dream present? If, say, the patient is due to have a test which he is afraid he might fail, then if the college goes up in flames, his test will be cancelled. Unconscious desire is not averse to exact a high toll in achieving realisation. In fact: the more extravagant the price, the better disguised is the desire. Similarly, a patient who went for a run every morning dreamt that she was forced to pass right through a house in the middle of a run, and of course it transpired she couldn't get out. It would be a mistake to interpret the main actress' frustration at being unable to get out of this labyrinth. This frustration only acts like a screen to the realised wish to stop running. As said, desire is embodied in the assumptions behind the dream narrative (the assumption that the morning-run was cancelled for reasons that have nothing to do with her). Desire may also occur outside the dream—like Freud's patient's desire to prove him wrong, or the desire, typical of nightmares, to wake up and discover it has only been a dream. In other cases, one may actually dream that one is dreaming. Often, this awareness of the dream being just that leads to immediate awakening—but this is not always the case. Freud regards dreaming about dreaming as a double defence (Freud, 1900a, p. 338). If the appearance of the wish as a dream constitutes a defence that allows the patient to say, "It's just a dream", then a dream within a dream is a double defence against knowing the wish. Another way of thinking about nightmares is that they are dreams in which the price of camouflaging the wish grows to the point of terror (the college burning down, for instance). By this logic, the more nightmarish the dream, the more repressed the wish. Nightmares, needless to say, also follow other types of logic, for instance the pleasure of the drive (for instance, the sadistic-pyromaniac impulse in the burning college dream).

From a technical perspective, Freud suggested that once the patient has recounted the remembered dream, he be asked to repeat it. The analyst pays close attention to any details that did not appear in the first account but emerged in the second. These details, even if they may appear marginal, are considered important because they are likely to have been repressed. It is to these details we shall ask the patient to associate (Freud, 1900a, pp. 96–121).

As regards dream images, what must be deciphered is the verbal expression concealed in the image, not its meaning or the feeling it arouses (Freud, 1900a, p. 49). Usually, feelings are the conscious response to the image, as the conscious mind understands the meaning of the image. A patient dreamt that his father was walking around with a music stand. This image aroused feelings of curiosity since his father had nothing to do with music. It could erroneously be concluded that curiosity about the father was the issue. Later in the same session, however, the patient used the expression: "he took a stand", and it transpired that this was the expression concealed in the music stand image. This is what Freud had in mind when he said that dream images must be deciphered as we decipher a rebus, a riddle in the form of shapes which represents expressions. When given due attention, the expression "he took a stand" caused the patient to be flooded by admiration for his father who stuck to his views, and by a sense of his own failure to meet this standard. The feeling realised-encoded by the dream was love: admiration for the father.

The theory and praxis of dream interpretation is also relevant for the interpretation of day dreams, stories, art, and the work produced in art therapy. It should be noted, however, that interpreting a work of art with a view to capturing the desire it enfolds is bound to put a clamp on creativity, much like the interpretation of jokes robs them of their humorous effect. Sometimes it is better not to analyse a work of art, which is an aim unto itself.

Moving to the couch as an act of interpretation

Historically, the couch was introduced because Freud felt uneasy about constantly being under his patients' gaze. The transition equally released the patient from eye contact which had also kept the encounter somewhat similar to any other friendly meeting. The couch affords both analyst and patient a freedom by not having to maintain a certain image. The analyst no longer needs to wear a certain expression (which obviously affects and is affected by his thoughts) or to be concerned about how he looks, and this helps him maintain his free floating, unfocused attention. As for the patient, the absence of eye contact also allows him to think of the analyst according to his unconscious fantasy (bored, angry, enjoying or forgiving). And so, the couch is really a kind of laboratory, whose conditions allow for recognition that the patient's assumptions regarding the analyst, and in general, are only just that: assumptions, whose origins are worth investigation.

Again, we should remember that only few therapies start off with analysis: most of them begin as psychotherapy, and the transition to the couch is neither obvious nor anticipated. The move is made as an act of interpretation. And like any interpretation, it is grounded in things the patient has said and it indicates desire (to move to the couch, in this case). If the patient for instance says he's tired; asks what the couch is for; mentions that it's difficult being in the other's eye; complains about being stuck in the intersubjective dimension ("I keep thinking about what you think about what I think")—in all these cases one can suggest the patient's request might be met by moving to the couch.

Cutting the session as an act of interpretation

It may well be that the analyst's practice of cutting the session is the most controversial issue in Lacanian psychoanalysis. There is a good reason for this: the cut is the very essence of the difference between the various types of post-Freudian analysis and Lacanian psychoanalysis. The common notion of the "short session" is inaccurate for the cut may occur after twenty minutes or after forty. The point is that the end time of the session cannot be known in advance—neither to the analyst nor to the patient.

The most powerful interpretation the analyst has available, the one that opens the unconscious, releasing associations, new insights, and positioning, is this act of cutting the session. One objective of the cut is to encourage thought between meetings. The patient's thoughts about things he would like to discuss in the treatment are an important part of the treatment. In so far as it functions to trigger a process, the session's main import lies in opening up thought and setting free association into motion, not in its duration. For this purpose, the point at which the session ends is critical due to the nature of speech, which may conceal no less than it reveals. Concealment, in the context of therapy, supports the patient's avoidance of taking a position or keeping that position unclear. The cut, in other words, blocks the escape route of the patient's defences. Thus, cutting a session with a depressive patient is likely to spark a demand, thereby revealing the manipulation which often lurks behind the depression and the desire that hides behind anger. When a patient says that it's all useless, that treatment isn't helping him, cutting the session at that point is likely to arouse his fury, showing that there are things he feels important enough to say.

In addition to deciding the patient's last statement, cutting the session also serves as a broader type of interpretation (Fink, 2007, p. 47). The cut has an enigmatic effect and this entails an experience of desire: the therapist's will arouses wonder and curiosity. The very mystery of the will of the person in the position of the big Other undermines any struggle arising in the face of this demand, exactly because the demand is unclear. Though the enigma may cause the patient to experience overwhelming anguish it is a necessary stage on the way from demand to desire. In the case of patients with neuroses, the enigma helps them to relax their rigid view of things (in the case of psychotic patients, however, it may dangerously encourage them to generate delusional explanations). The cut has the additional effect of prompting the patient to say what's important to him and to decide what's trivial. Neurotic patients will engage in chatter in an attempt to avoid their desire. This is why they often raise what really matters toward the end of the session, as if they were dropping the bomb right before they go. Knowing that time is limited and that no matter what, he will not be able to say everything, encourages the patient to express what's really meaningful in a radical manner. The patient starts with what is most pressing because the session may come to a close before he's managed to mention it.

Lacan mentions another aspect of the cut, namely that it gets in the way of confabulation and the illusions of knowledge. It prevents speech from becoming based on the pleasure of speech for its own sake or on the phantasmatic experience that we understand what we are saying—i.e., on an imaginary agreement (Lacan, 1978 [1963], p. 250). Because the aim of treatment, in many ways, is to forego the gratification of jouissance in order to make place for desire, will and ambition which are fundamental to action, speech itself is bound to produce a jouissance that is an obstacle to action. People often come to treatment to get help in moving on to action: speech indeed brings us closer to the edge of the cliff of action but it is not part of the act of jumping. To get from speech to action, a quantum leap is necessary: the act will be done on condition that speech stops. Cutting the session facilitates this shift by putting a halt to the jouissance of speech which could substitute for action ad infinitum. No matter how much the patient would like to say more, the cut helps him recognise that not everything can be said, and that if he delays action in order to put it all into words, he will never do anything.

The cut reflects the psychoanalyst's ethical commitment to the patient's desire. While in other types of treatment, the therapist, at the end of the pre-set fifty minutes wraps up the patient's unconscious before the latter goes back into the world, the analyst in Lacanian psychoanalysis is obliged to be constantly alert to make the cut at the most opportune moment. The obsessive-normative structure of the fifty-minute session is bound to exempt the therapist from taking a position and instead to bolster the patient's faith in normalcy. In his everyday life, too, the patient probably makes decisions on the basis of arbitrary rules and norms. If the duration of the session is not determined by a norm—then by what is it determined? By the same thing we would like to guide all of our choices: desire. The position of the analyst when he makes the interpretation that cuts the session is a position regarding the patient's unconscious desire. If the patient concludes a certain topic by saying: "That's it!" the analyst cuts as though he interpreted: "When you say: 'That's it!' it is your wish to end the session, and I respect your wish." The thought about the twenty minutes remaining until the end of the fifty-minute session is like a demand or a command which it is the treatment's objective to undo. If in session that is based on fifty minutes it is the norm that rules, in a session whose duration is based on the patient's speech it is the word of the subject of the unconscious that rules. The interpretation of the analyst has the following meaning: "You are your own and only master."

CHAPTER THREE

Transference

Transference in the Freudian sense

Transference can be delineated in two ways. Freud and early Lacan referred to the transferal onto the analyst of feelings of love or hate which were originally aimed at significant people (usually the parents) in the subject's life. In this sense, transference is associated with repetition. The patient revisits scenes from the past, casting the analyst in the role of one of the historical figures. To illustrate: a patient who feels the victim of his father will reproduce scenes of past victimhood with the analyst (Freud, 1914g, p. 151).

There is an element of defensiveness in transference. Repeating past experience turns the encounter with the other into something that seems transparent. The other's will becomes a thing foreseen (exploitation, for instance). This fictive certainty offers a kind of foil against coping with the enigma of the other's desire—something that arouses distress. The patient ascribes a certain demand to the analyst in order to protect himself against not knowing the former's desire. The patient, not knowing who he may be for the analyst, has to confront the question of what the analyst may want of him. This is where historic transference has a soothing influence: it enables the patient to believe he knows what's expected of him (Freud, 1914g, pp. 101–107).

Transference is likely to set in even before the first session, as the patient imagines who the analyst may be. Often, transference motivates the choice of analyst—and this is just as well, because it is on the basis of the transference that treatment works. Release from old relational patterns can only be achieved if they are reproduced to begin with. The very fact that the analyst listens to the patient is enough to make the transference happen. That it is his role to listen suffices to prevent him from pouring too much of his own contents into the relationship, constituting him as a *tabula rasa* for the patient's projections. When the patient lies on the couch and does not see the analyst this effect is even stronger. In that position, he can attribute anything to the analyst.

Transference and identification

Freudian transference is based on identification. Having devoted a year-long seminar to the subject, Lacan often repeated how important identification is to analytic work and that it always passes through the other. In the transference, an early position of the patient reappears taking one of Freud's three forms of identification. The first of these is identification as a highly valuable primordial phallic object which supplements the other (the object that supplements the mother, for example). Identification with an ideology, religion, or community also derives from this same identification as the supplementary object, as, indeed, does the refusal to belong (by adding a minus) (Freud, 1921c, pp. 105–107).

The second form of identification, according to Freud, is with the parents and it occurs by means of adopting a common feature (hairstyle, high heels). Lacan is particularly intrigued by this identification through a feature or marker because he considers it a proto-signifier or prototype of the signifier. The human subject for him, is a linguistic creature, who is essentially constituted by the signifier—which is based on the identity marker.

The third type of identification is hysterical—here identification is with the other's desire. Freud describes how in a residential school for girls all the girls cried in response to a goodbye letter one of them received from her boyfriend: as if he had abandoned all of them. In hysterical identification, the other's desire serves as a feature of identification by means of which the subject knows herself.

A main objective in Lacanian treatment with people who suffer from neurosis is to free them from identifications (Lacan, 1978 [1963], p. 274). Some symptoms function like identity markers: an organically unexplained limp turned out to be a way of identifying with a father whose leg had been amputated. Identification by way of a supplementary object for the other is a formative component of neurotic symptoms, as neurosis—more or less by definition—is the tendency to follow norms from the belief that they are the true or imaginary expectations of significant others. Hysterical identification, for example, functions as a demand to obey others' wishes. It is under its auspices that someone may only feel attracted to his partner if he can think of her as attractive to others (with whose attraction he can identify). Identification with the object and hysterical identification with the other's desire come together where a person wants something because this is what other people expected her to want. For example, one father who brought his five-year-old son in for treatment because he was hurting other children in playschool, said: "So who cares whether he's the strongest kid in school? Does that mean he should be hitting others?" The child smiled as the father was saying this, disclosing his identification with the aggressive wish the father would like him to cary and fulfil. The fact that neither father nor son was conscious of what was going on only further enhances the impossibility of choosing differently.

If we agree that it is in the nature of desire as a product of language, to come from the other (Lacan, 2002 [1958a], pp. 518–537), how can we pinpoint those desires that are faithful to the subject? The answer comes only after the event: they are the desires that will persist, that will result in symptoms and distress when left unexpressed. In treatment, the question of identification arises in the context of symptoms, as the factor that underlies the latter. The analyst's attention, in this case, is informed by questions about what the patient is defending herself against when she sticks to an identification and acts according to it, and what meaning this identification supports. A patient, for instance, sought treatment complaining that he found it hard to maintain a long-term relationship. It transpired that he was enacting the role of the ultimate seducer of many women in order to meet his mother's expectations. Acquitting himself of this identification as his mother's object released him from its ordained tight hold. This identification's repetition in the transference will manifest itself when it is possible to interpret that the patient relates to the analyst as the mother whose pride he is trying to arouse.

The Lacanian notion of transference

If the first type of transference, being a return to past identifications and relations, is essentially biographical, then the second type of transference is structural as it reflects the structure of the patient's unconscious. The repetition of patterns from the past doesn't allow change. Had there only been transference of the first kind, treatment would not feature new phenomena—only reproductions of past emotions and relations. This, though, is not the case. In the treatment both positive and negative feelings emerge as a result of the fact that the patient assumes the analyst has knowledge, something that is entailed by the very structure of the therapeutic relations. The link to childhood experience, that is, is not necessary. Triggering transference by means of taking an enigmatic position, the analyst positions herself as someone whose desire is unclear. She causes the patient to wonder about her desire, by enigmatic talk or by sidestepping questions. This obscurity is aimed to stir the sexual unconscious: sexual in the primordial sense, dating back to infancy when sexuality and love were inextricable. When a man says about a woman, "She knows me better than I know myself" he actually says he loves her. Similarly, in psychoanalysis, when we refer knowledge about ourselves to the other, we feel love—transference, in other words.

In his seminar on transference, Lacan analyses Plato's *Symposium* to deepen his understanding of transference love. Alcibiades loves Socrates yet Socrates, like the psychoanalyst, is reluctant to identify himself with the image of the loved one. What Alcibiades in fact loves, he argues, is the *agalma*, a hidden treasure which he attributes to Socrates (Lacan, 1960, session 6). *Agalma*, it becomes clear by the end of the dialogue, is desire itself, in other words: the object of desire is desire itself—not the appearance of the Imaginary Other: ideal, admired, or authoritarian. What Alciabiades, then, loves about Socrates is that Socrates loves. Desire attracts desire.

In a love relationship—unlike in Lacanian oriented treatment—the emptiness of *agalma* remains unrevealed. Love is blind to the fact that attraction derives not from the object, the figure of love's object, but from its enigmatic nature. Since the object of desire is desire itself—an inversion occurs in relations of love: The one who attracts is attractive by virtue of being attracted, or in other words: the one who loves becomes beloved. Where there is a relationship of love, *agalma* manifests itself when the loved one declares his love. Socrates' analytical position puts him in the place of the loved one, of the object—he remains enigmatic, that is, doesn't become a lover himself, his love remains unclarified. If the analyst would meet the patient's demand to be loved, this would make it impossible for the patient to continue discovering her or his ability to love. Since treatment aims to allow the patient to love, the analyst must be willing to be loved by means of keeping an enigmatic position.

A dialectic of truth

Simply said, positive transference occurs where analysts, doing their work faithfully, seek the truth of their patients' desire. Patients will eventually love their analyst for insisting that they must not avoid their desires and forego responsibility for their choices. The dialectic of truth is a term Lacan uses when describing Freud's treatment of Dora (Lacan, 1985, p. 61). Analysts' willingness to acknowledge the biographical truth of an other's responsibility for the patient's condition—a truth denied by the patient's surroundings—paves the way for the structural truth about the patient's choices, desires and pleasure as a subject. Using the trust thus gained in order to cast doubt on certain contradictions in the patient's position, they lead the patient to recognise unconscious desires. Freud, for instance, agreed with Dora's anger at her father for having exploited her when he urged her to spend time with Mr K by way of clearing the scene for his own affair with Mrs K in the meantime. Freud then used the trust gained by not pretending innocence about her father, when confronting Dora on her choice to go along with this situation. Thus, Freud could confirm her complaint on the one hand while also pointing out her collusion on the other. Her desire to position herself as a desireless victim is a hysteric desire.

Analysts embroider their work by means of positive transference. The dialectic of truth encourages positive transference, as said, in the form of love of someone who knows more about the patient than she or he himself, and who will not let the latter relinquish their truth. Dialectic interpretation is equally relevant of course where it concerns patients' attitude to their analyst. An analyst, thus, may suggest that a patient is trying to manoeuvre him into the position of a figure from the latter's past. In an earlier mentioned illustration (see Chapter One), for instance, a patient asks his analyst: "Do you think I should stop drinking when I drive?" The obvious response would be to insist the patient stop it, but a response that interprets the transference might look something like this: "I'm sorry you have no father". This response rather than meeting the demand by posing a counter-demand, interprets the concealed desire. Instead of entering the negative transference of the neglectful or demanding father on the lines of Freudian transference, the analyst points at the truth of the patient's desire, triggering positive transference in the Lacanian sense. Freud might actually have responded similarly by refusing the transference directed at him, but rather than considering this a refusal of transference, Lacan would think of it as a transition to structural transference.

We might wish to add that the analyst's use of the personal pronoun "I" is likely to hold up the impression that the person to whom the patient refers is the actual analyst as a subject. If an analyst says, "You love me/are angry with me" she may be falling in with the appearances of the transference, according to which the patient's feelings are addressed to a person who is the analyst, rather than to the transferential figure located in the analyst. Often, therefore, analysts' reference to themselves can be left out. So, for example, rather than saying, "I think you're being evasive", they might ask: "Are you being evasive?" This stance may also help analysts cope better with the emotional turbulence to which they are exposed as a result of patients' directing their emotions at them.

Resistance and defence

For Freud, transference as such is a form of resistance which must be overcome on the way to truth. Lacan further focuses this by adding that the object of resistance is the renunciation of jouissance. If an analyst takes a position regarding the patient's jouissance—say by berating the latter, even if only indirectly, for her angry outbursts—then it is reasonable to expect that the patient will react with acting out. In taking a stance, i.e., in speaking in behalf of a norm or law, the analyst fails to observe her role which is not to negate jouissance. Lacan argues that resistance can only originate in the analyst. If a patient is late, stops coming in for meetings, attacks the analyst, and so on, it is safe to assume the analyst has been urging the patient to surrender a pleasure.

One component of the freedom necessary for psychoanalytic work is the freedom from taking a position. When it happens that an analyst resists a patient's jouissance, he must ask himself why he resists, where has he possibly left his own analysis unfinished? Lacan argues that Freud was wrong when he tried to persuade a young homosexual woman to go out with men, or told Dora to stop turning away from Mr K—these acts were the outcome of his heterosexual and marital ideals. When an analyst objects to murder or paedophilia he does so in his capacity of being a member of western civilisation and a professional who was licensed by the state—not as part of his analytic stance. Psychoanalysis, in this sense, cannot be pure. Since the psychoanalyst does not identify with the law, he needs the law at his side.

As opposed to resistance—which is, as said, resistance to giving up jouissance—a defence resists knowledge of a desire, i.e., the removal of repression (Lacan, 1966, session 6). Here analysts take a clear position supporting the removal of defences in favour of exposing unconscious desires (with the clinical caveat to keep in mind patients' phase of treatment). For this purpose, they will stay with their patients without trying too much to allay their anxiety, since anxiety is a typical response to desire when it is about to become conscious.

Jouissance and defence intertwine as repression comes with inherent jouissance. This is the one jouissance which analysts resist in their analytic role. Here transference love is crucial because it enables patients to tolerate the anxiety of setting aside repression's jouissance. "Only love allows jouissance to condescend to desire", said Lacan (1962, session 14). It is only where they attribute knowledge to, and have trust in, their analyst that patients will be capable of resigning the pleasures of resistance and defence for the sake of knowing their desire.

Treatment is likely to be time consuming. Interpretations given in the past are bound to become clear or take effect only with the passing of time, when patients are willing to know. Analysts must respect patients' right not to know. They will provide their patients with cues that enable them to know, should they be ready. Interpretations, like symptoms, are in this sense hints for those who choose to know.

CHAPTER FOUR

Symptom

In the medical context, the symptom points at illness: in psychoanalysis it points at the unconscious. Like slips of the tongue, dreams or jokes, the symptom is one of the ways the unconscious expresses itself. The symptom, one could say, is what brings the patient to treatment in hopes that the analyst will understand it. Here I will discuss some ways in which we may understand what the symptom is and how it functions for the subject.

The symptom as an outcome that supports an assumption

Simple logic rests on assumptions (e.g., that the sun rises in the east and sets in the west) which have outcomes and implications (Paris time is one hour earlier than time in Jerusalem). The logic of the symptom works in the opposite direction. It relies on the invention of an outcome to constitute a certain assumption with hindsight—guilt, for instance, about not having attended a certain event, which supports the assumption that my presence there is critical. The symptom, in short, comes to shore up a certain assumption by establishing itself as the outcome of this assumption (Lacan, 2002 [1960], pp. 681–682).

From this perspective, the main question the analyst faces concerning the symptom is what reality it constructs for the person in question; how does this way of thinking serve her or him? The above logic suggests that, being an external constraint, one that supposedly was not chosen by the subject, the symptom allows the person to yearn or desire without having to take responsibility for this choice. There's a joke about a Jew in the Wild West, who found himself seated among gunmen who were passing round a bottle of whisky. When the bottle reached him, the Jew declined, explaining that the whisky was not kosher. When one of the men told him, at gunpoint, to drink or else, the Jew answered: "If you're pointing the gun already, why not pass me the pork while you're at it?" The paradigmatic structure of the symptom is: "It's not my fault that I am enjoying: I was forced to." Guilt, similarly, maintains the assumption: "I am guilty in the face of authority, therefore there is someone to feel guilty toward, therefore I am not an orphan." And there is another component of guilt which I think is important: Guilt also serves as a pretext for enjoying pleasures (I did something wrong but I feel guilty so it's OK).

The symptom as the bastion of the subject's singularity

Symptoms develop and get entrenched the more adaptive and normative patients try to be in disregard of their desires. The more the soldier believes he must follow orders and resist his urges, the more he will get in trouble because of forgetting to wear his beret.

In this sense, the symptom is the unconscious' insistence on singularity in the face of the subject's refusal to stand behind (or identify with) that singularity—that is: to be willing to pay a price. So, if the symptom sustains desire, the analyst choose the side of the symptom rather than that of adaptation. Analysts are "in favour" of the symptom, or rather: in favour of the desire it represents. Once the subject embraces it the symptom becomes superfluous. The message of Lacanian analysis is as follows: "Freud insists on it from the start, a way of acknowledging where alone, the acknowledgement is possible because the Imaginary is the place where all truth is stated and a truth denied has just as much Imaginary weight as an acknowledged truth" (Lacan, 1974, p. 130). It is as if the subject were saying: If I refuse it then I can believe it is a possibility. If identification were a fantasy, there would be no need to defend against it with symptomatic singularity. This makes the wrapping of desire in symptoms superfluous.

By virtue of its distance from the source, the symptom, like metaphor or a fable, is an effective formulation of truth; it is a structure that represents the subject by means of an object (Lacan, 2002 [1957], p. 435). So a boy who feels his parents don't let him be may develop constipation by way of a symptom, as if he was using a metaphor: "The thing does not get out of the system", with his excrement standing in for himself.

Claude Levi-Strauss' structuralist theory uses the concept of metaphor to cast light on the relations between various systems, organised by means of a totemic method, operative among Amazonian tribes. Until then, functionalist anthropologists had thought of the totem as an object of identification (for instance, the jaguar as the forefather with whom the tribe identifies on account of, say, its daring). Levi-Strauss argued that the role of the totem is rooted in myths including ones that describe and regulate the relations between the totems of various tribes (Levi-Strauss, 1962, p. 19).

A similar logic can be distinguished in the workings of the symptom. A hysterical symptom, for instance, uses the body as though it were a myth that was telling a story. A patient complains of pains, pointing at a spot roughly between his hip and shoulder. When asked to name the place, he says "In my side". At some point in the course of the meeting he had said the following: "I find it hard not to have affairs on the side." Once the analyst made the connection between the side pain and this statement, the pain stopped. Likewise, one day as I was driving my car, I had a sudden spasm in my throat. Wondering whether what was happening to me was a symptom, an expression of my unconscious, I tried to trace back my thoughts up till that moment. The radio had been reporting on people being killed in a terror attack, and earlier that same morning, I heard that a person I knew had died of cardiac arrest. Next, I thought that he wasn't even that old and that it could happen to any one of us, unannounced, and that the knowledge that we can die any moment is "like a knife at my throat". Recollecting this thought caused my throat to relax immediately. As long as I repressed my fear of death, my unconscious represented the intolerable knowledge by means of the body rather than through consciousness. The body declared "knife at my throat" instead of it being consciously expressed in words. Once consciousness took in the knowledge, the symptom of the throat spasm vanished. Just as the mythic world of animals and plants serves as a metaphor for the tribe's social life, the human body and the names of its parts function as a metaphor for the mind and its drives.

The conceptualisations of the symptom which I have so far presented relate to it as a coded message that can be deciphered (provided there's a willingness to hear). Freud insisted that the symptom itself includes information about the drive: the symptom is a type of compromise between repression and expression. In the symptom, in this sense, two opposing states are sustained simultaneously. So, for instance, an obsessive person who constantly cleans the toilet driven by an urge for hygiene, in actual fact spends most of his days with his hand in the toilet bowl. He tries, by way of the symbol of physical cleanliness, to clean away something of his mental impulses. Obviously, it does not work. In Shakespeare's play, Lady Macbeth tries to concretely wash off the symbolic blood, the violence held in the expression "blood on her hands". When the symbolic solution is not adequate, the symptom is subsumed by compulsive action (which is why Lady Macbeth, for instance, washes her hands incessantly) (Freud, 1913m, p. 208). The existence of the urge is suggested by the symptom and it is open to the analyst's decoding. The object of this decoding is the drive's subject as the latter manifests her or himself in the symptom. Patients deposit their symptom with the analyst, much like a letter can be deposited with the lawyer to be opened at some later point in time. As for now, they are not ready to cope with the knowledge, yet they don't want to simply forego it. Analysts' interpretations follow the symptom's pointers by offering patients the choice to know about their urges.

What follows is that the symptom takes the form of the story and its morale. Even if it were possible to dissolve the symptom (by exposing the desire it conceals and the subject's structure) this is not advisable from the perspective of the ethics of psychoanalysis. It would be like throwing out the baby with the bathwater. The ultimate morale is the Real and its story is the Symbolic. Much like in human consciousness, the morale has no existence other than through its manifestation in the story, the desiring subject cannot be but in the space between the Real and the Symbolic—i.e., the symptom. Hence the point of psychoanalysis is not to destroy the symptom together with the desires it encapsulates but rather to get the symbol to support the (Symbolic) subject in the face of (the Real) jouissance. Speeding on the road by way of a symptom, for instance, can function as the story for the morale: "Life is short—there's no time." If the person would take up racing as their hobby—say—they would be sustaining the symptom in a way that supports their subjectivity, their desire and its expressions—but in a conscious manner that allows to take ownership of this desire, avoiding the excessive price at whose cost desire is denied (on the lines of: "I am driving recklessly fast—not because I enjoy the speed but because I am late"). The Symbolic system can be seen as a super-symptom in the face of the Real; a symptom that supports the subject by enabling meaning and jouissance and desire at one and the same time. Analytical psychotherapy's aim is for the patient to take responsibility for her or his symptom and to make use of it. At the end of the treatment, the symptom no longer represents an illness but is a structure that supports the subject (Soler, 2003, p. 250–252).

That the symptom takes the shape of a complaint at the start of treatment is the result of its sustaining a metaphoric lack. But this metaphoric lack, in turn, sustains the subject in so far the latter follows the logic of "I lack therefore I am". The original, mythic lack thanks to which the subject exists is the lack of the Real, which is created by the Symbolic—in other words: the discrepancy between things as they are and the words that come to replace them. It is this inconceivable lack that the symptom represents through a variety of losses—such as a sense of inferiority or lack of satisfaction. While some (like Heidegger for instance) have argued that our fundamental sense of lack is inherent to the fact that we are mortal, Freud attributes it to sexual difference. Lacan argues that the first approach (lack as related to transience) is the hallmark of the obsessive personality structure, whereas the second (lack as related to sexual difference) marks the hysterical personality. For Lacan, the more basic lack is what emerges as a result of the gap between Real and Symbolic; the Real that vanishes with the appearance of the word, the gap between experience and expression. The mythical, original lost object cannot be represented other than by the symptom, a variation on the original lack. Hence there is no subject without symptom.

One definition Lacan gave of anguish is the absence of absence (the absence of the absence that would allow desire). If the symptom sustains absence or lack, then symptom and anguish alternate. Anguish will appear where the symptom does not work. A student who procrastinates in handing in his work sustains, in this manner, a gap between the requirement to write a paper and writing itself. Should the professor tell him he can deliver his paper whenever he wants—i.e., robbing him from the symptom that sustains lack or absence—the student will experience anguish. Similarly, anguish is bound to make itself felt the moment he has submitted his paper.

The symptom involves a certain protest by the subject in the face of the deceptiveness of the Symbolic: it isn't the real world, it crushes the Real. Neo, in the film "The Matrix", suffers from insomnia. His unconscious, it turns out, knows more than he can admit that he lives in a virtual world and the insomnia is a symptomatic response to this, a refusal to ignore this, to live in a stupor. This logic also suits the symptom of compulsive checking ("Did I lock the car?") or when a person who worries that she might forget something will tie a ribbon to her finger so as to remember, and then forgets what the ribbon was supposed to remind her of. So, she ties another ribbon in order to remind her of what the first ribbon should have reminded her, and so on. In the absence of something that will tie the ribbon to the real thing which it represents, every other ribbon hits the same obstacle. The person who locked his car refuses, unconsciously, to rely on his memory as what validates reality.

The Lacanian analyst cannot but agree with his patients that the Symbolic does not have the validity of the Real. Patients' grievance against the Symbolic is directed against their own wish that it should be valid in actuality. This is an internal conflict. As far as the analyst is concerned the problem lies with neurotic people's refusal to accept the truth that their symptom presents. Neurotic people's consciousness refuses to accept that it is impossible for the Real and the Symbolic to match—something which the unconscious insists on revealing by means of the symptom. Perceiving it through the Symbolic prism as a lost paradise, they refuse to surrender the pre-linguistic Real. In the face of this neurotic refusal to attend to the truth it embodies, the symptom persists. If we don't allow the obsessive person to check if he locked his car, he will experience anguish. While he appears to fear that his car may be stolen, the Lacanian perspective is that his distress is in response to the inability to validate the link between the Symbolic (memory) and the Real (the door) (Lacan, 1961, session 9). The hysterical person too, in his attempts to dismantle authority, to bring to light the human frailty of one would like to be the master, wishes to unfetter the Real from the Symbolic. Like the person who suffers from obsession he declines to acknowledge that the Real for which he exerts himself is nothing but another symbolical myth (the humanity of the master).

The suffering inherent in the symptom can be considered as a means for validating reality. It resembles, in this, what we do when we pinch ourselves in order to convince ourselves that the good feelings we experience in our dream are real. Pain takes the role of validation in all rites of passage and blood pacts. The symptom operates in the same way when validation is unconscious. This is why the analyst seeks to stay close to the symbolic reality which the pain aims to validate as being real. Reality will not validate the symbolic truth (which is what the neurotic subject believes): only the subject can confirm the desire the symptom embodies and reduce the suffering that goes under the guise of reality confirmation.

But not totally. To some extent the symptom is irreducible because beyond its role as significant example or message, it also includes a Real core that sustains it. Neither interpretation nor decoding is of any avail here. Some jouissance comes with symptomatic suffering, with its excitement, a mysterious root of masochism which Freud investigated among people suffering from shell shock, and which can be found in more trivial forms of excitement too. Here is where Freudian psychoanalysis approaches its point of exhaustion, where there is no sense in continuing interpretation, where change in the symptom dwindles and a remainder of Real jouissance persists. This is not of the person's choice and all she or he can do when she encounters it is to accept, that is: to identify with the symptom rather than to resist it (Soler, 2003, pp. 250–252).

Ellen Degeneres has a stand-up act where she begins with confessing to, and apologising for, being a procrastinator, and ends up identifying herself proudly as a procrastinator, that is, someone who does what she wants. At the early stages of treatment the patient makes a mistake and turns left instead of right. Later she begins to regard it as a Freudian mistake and see what it is that she wants on that left turn. When she identifies with the symptom and the jouissance it encapsulates, she turns left by way of a choice and the original right turn as the ideal choice impostering as desire.

Symptom and phantasm

English translations of Lacan maintain the notion of the *phantasm* (*phantasme* is French for fantasy) as such in in order to convey his distinct use of the term. If with the entry of the symbol the subject became split, lacking and yearning, the phantasm produces an image of mythic wholeness restored. In spite of its inherent failure—after all, it too is composed of signifiers—the phantasmatic myth upholds jouissance in the form of a semblance of wholeness, the discovery of the lost object and its return to its proper place.

The phantasm involves a subject and an object and the gap between them, and it occurs as a circumscribed event with a beginning and an end. Unlike the symptom (about which the patient usually complains explicitly) the phantasm is secret and its discovery by the analyst tends to involve embarrassment. Its most articulate manifestation, when it rises to consciousness, is the orgasmic sexual fantasy (Lacan, 1978 [1963], p. 185). More often, the phantasm lies concealed behind an associative chain of signifiers. Freud extracted the Rat Man's fundamental phantasm from his story—recounted with a shocked expression on his face—about the insertion of a rat into the anal cavity as an act of torture. Freud unravelled the symbolic logic of this phantasm: The German word for rat (*Ratten*) is homophonic with the word for payment (*Raten*). Since money symbolises excrement, putting a rat into the anal cavity bears out his father's returning of a debt to a creditor, and—on a deeper stratum—restoring the lost anal object to the body (Freud, 1909d, p. 213).

Lost objects are not only returned in the context of the body. Every phantasm originates in the desire for fusion with the mother, which relieves the subject from the burden of separation. If, in the case of the Rat Man, the latter occupies the place of the subject and excrement is the object, in the phantasm of incest, it is the mother who takes the role of subject and the one who has the phantasy features as object (Lacan, 1966, session 12). A variety of objects may take the role of the phantasmatic object, and the gaze is one of these. One patient told how he secretly spied on a woman and when she noticed him he fainted. The naked woman, or parts of her body, would appear to be the object here. Since however the voyeur's jouissance depends on the woman's unawareness of being observed (he does not get similarly excited by watching a stripper), it transpires that the gaze is his object of pleasure. The gaze (his) is the hidden object of jouissance from the start. When her gaze falls on him and exposes his gaze, he faints for sheer pleasure. The gap between his knowing and her innocence functions as a metaphor for the gap between subject and object, between organ and body, between child and mother. When the gazes cross, the gap of yearning collapses and jouissance overflows and the subject, fainting, vanishes within it.

The cut, the symbolic element that separates subject from object, is an integral part of the phantasm. Pleasure from phantasy derives from the symbolic element, i.e., the signifier, for it is the story of completing the lack, rather than actual completion that generates jouissance. The gap between subject and object—opening and closing by turns—is clearly present in the dynamic of addiction. The object of addiction is not simply or only satisfaction, but the phantasmatic cycle as such, based as it is in the cyclic repetition of loss and recovery, yearning and satisfaction. This is the reason, for instance, why people who want to give up smoking don't rush to take pills that suppress the need to smoke. What they find hard is to give up the desire, as the phantasm paradoxically upholds desire as a form of jouissance.

Psychoanalytic attention aims to identify in symptoms the root of the phantasm and the pleasure it yields. In demeaning arguments between spouses, one might pinpoint a sado-masochistic phantasm which has spilled out of the sexual scene. Even as noticing the camera when it enters the frame as we watch a film will spoil our pleasure, awareness of the fact that these arguments are a game is bound to undermine the pleasure they yield. Where jouissance is excessive and unconscious, the analyst may manoeuvre the camera into the frame by showing the patient how he stages the phantasm in which he unconsciously participates. This process of growing aware and free of the phantasm Lacan called "crossing the phantasm" (1978 [1963], p. 273).

The difference between fantasies and the phantasm is that fantasies about a promised wholeness can be many, but the subject's formative phantasm is one and, also in contrast to many fantasies, it is unconscious. While fantasies can function as a tool by means of which the subject takes conscious pleasure, the unconscious phantasm can determine the subject's mode of conduct without his or her knowledge and thus cause much suffering. The basic masochistic phantasm, for instance, is that of being a cast off object. This encapsulates a compromise between the wish to be whole (the object, as opposed to the subject, is whole), yet, nevertheless, to be free of the mother's body, and hence: cast off. Signs of masochism, like pain, humiliation, or rejection are nothing but representations of "I am cast off therefore I am free". Once there is recognition of the phantasmatic root "cast off object" in the symptom of "being rejected", there is no more need to take the position of being rejected in order to be free.

CHAPTER FIVE

Trauma, anguish, and depression

Trauma

An event is traumatic if it rends the fragile texture of the Symbolic order. Exposure to the reality of a body maimed in a road accident reveals the virtuality of the Symbolic reality. Fundamental notions about human beings—that they have stable and enduring external form, a face, a name, characteristics, a role—collapse. Medics and emergency teams have an extensive symbolic repertoire (concept, roles) to protect them against the experience of meaninglessness associated with trauma. The tendency to repeat typical of those who have experienced trauma can be understood in terms of the unconscious in search of the words that will enable it to mentalise the trauma. The experience keeps being reproduced in all its actuality because it does not translate well enough into the Symbolic dimension. Horror images keep returning in a hopeless effort to become conceptualised or part of thought (Lacan, 1988 [1954], p. 85).

Therapeutic work with trauma aims to fix the tear in the Symbolic by means of recounting the event in different, ever more comprehensive contexts. A patient, for example, who witnessed his comrades dead in battle will talk about the event in a circular manner: what led up to the event, what happened there, what happened afterwards, the broader context of the trauma, the military constellation in the region, the geopolitical conditions of war, and so on. Treatment must put a tragic frame on the trauma (Boothby, 1991, p. 202), to give meaning when symbolic meaning collapsed. Though the tragic hero fails to realise his plans or wishes we nevertheless experience catharsis because the experience of loss is framed symbolically. "It could not have happened differently", or "It was written in the stars" refer to something that did not happen senselessly, that was part of a narrative—whether divine, cosmic or historical. Fate, which we know we have to accept, belongs in a system which also offers poetic justice by way of compensation, maintaining a narrative perception of life. This is also how rituals of remembrance work, like memorial days: they put the trauma in a tragic context by wrapping it in esthetic-symbolical layers like song and music. Trauma repeats itself continuously, it exists in an enduring present. The Symbolic dimension allow the insertion of the temporal—thereby transforming the trauma into memory, something that has been.

Psychoanalysis, that owes its particularity to Freud's putting responsibility on the subject of the unconscious, is in no rush to absolve subjects from responsibility for the unconscious phantasm concealed in the event which is ostensibly external to them. Slavoj Žižek, the Lacanian theoretician, infuriated many when he revealed the hidden jouissance of 9/11, making its appearance in cinematic images even prior to 2001 (Žižek, 2002). The Lacanian notion of the Real has two meanings. One refers to the libido that is not symbolically channelled and hence remains extraneous to individuals' subjectivity. The other points at external catastrophes like natural disasters. Catastrophe and libido join wherever the former is manmade—like for instance the Holocaust.

Yekhiel Dinur, also known as the writer Ka-Tzetnik, wrote about his experience in the Holocaust. In his book Ztofen Edma which unfortunately was not translated from Hebrew to English tells about receiving a treatment against insomnia which worked by means of inducing an LSD trance. In the wake of this treatment he changed his mind about seeing the Holocaust as a Nazi phenomenon—instead he came to regard it as a human phenomenon. In the trance he saw himself in Nazi uniform. In addition to recognising the horrors of the Real, he perceived a drive he didn't lack either. Once he no longer needed to escape his own drives, Ka-Tzetnik recovered his sleep. In addition to subduing the Real by means of its translation into the Symbolic system, the treatment of trauma also subjectivises it. This implies that the subject takes responsibility for and ownership of the Real of the jouissance that inhabits her or him. Here Lacan is more faithful to Freud than most of his other followers who stopped dealing with the concept of the death drive.

Anguish

Anguish, like trauma, is linked to the encounter with the Real entailing loss of the symbol, but it is both less violent and potentially of much clinical value. Lacan decided to translate the German *Angst*, which Freud used, with *anguish* rather than with *anxiety*, Strachey's choice. Anguish is essentially an experience of excess (Chouraqui-Sepel, 2005), (something Lacan referred to as "the lack of the lack"). As said, desire relies on lack; the meaning of yearning is that an object of lack is formulated and designated as the object of desire. Anguish is a state of fullness and hence it excludes desire, since in this situation no object of lack can be appointed (as an object of desire, that is) (Fink, 1997, pp. 177–178). While Freud considers anguish as a sign of danger (whether internal or external), Lacan perceives it as threatening the subject with the eradication of lack, the eradication, that is, of yearning, including subjectivity itself which depends on lack.

In the course of their development children invest their sexual energy, or libido, in various objects: the mother's breast, the mother, their own person, objects in or on their body and elsewhere—as part of a process one might call fetishisation. More radical would be the argument that it is this very investment that creates the objects-signifiers (Lacan, 1966, session 1), in the sense that the libidinal investment institutes both object and urge. It is thanks to the process of fetishisation that the subject's desire participates in the libidinal exchange market between objects (that is to say: from the mother to the transitional object, and next to various other objects).

Unlike depression, where libido gets attached to a lost object (as Freud described it in his essay "Mourning and Melancholia"), in the case of anguish the object is not lost but has not yet become separate as such by means of libidinal investment. Uninvested into an object, the libido is experienced as oppressive excess (of jouissance). This aimless wandering through the body can be stopped when the libido is channelled into a well-defined object which exists in the world of images and language, an object with a name, that is. This is why putting an experience into words helps to alleviate anguish. In a similar manner, the symptom too offers release from anguish—it links jouissance to an object (if a fetishist is not given access to her object she will experience anguish). Differently put: the symptom sustains lack (as I explained earlier).

Earlier in his career, Freud considered anguish as an outcome of repression. If someone represses the knowledge that her partner is betraying her, discovering the betrayal—i.e., removal of the repression—will make her feel lighter. In his later work, *Inhibitions, Symptoms and Anxiety*, Freud changed his mind and rather than conceiving of anguish as a response only to repressed signifiers and meanings, he now saw it as a response to lack of meaning, too, similar to a traumatic situation (Freud, 1926d). Agreeing with both versions, Lacan emphasises anguish as a response to paradox, to the collapse of logic and the symbolic structures it supports. Freud's concept of *"das Unheimliche"*—the uncanny—which arises where the repressed returns, illustrates this (Freud, 1919h, pp. 237–240). Here something is experienced as remote and near simultaneously. When a child is afraid of a monster, for instance, his fear originates in his own drives which he experiences as wholly alien (Lacan,1962, session 6). All paradox derives from one fundamental paradox which cancels the differences between inside and outside. When one encounters such structures, the experience is one of disorientation, much like the feeling one gets looking at M. C. Escher's drawings. This perplexity is what Lacan identified as the essence of anguish.

In his article on the uncanny, Freud refers to E. T. A. Hoffmann's horror story "The devil's elixirs", which features a hero whose eyes have been gouged out and who holds an eyeball in his hand that stares back at him. Over and beyond the shocking image of the gouged-out eyeball with its overtones of Freudian castration, Lacan draws our attention to how this scene seriously subverts logic. The eye cannot see if it isn't connected to the brain. And one cannot observe the eye without the gouged-out eye. This scenario puts our most fundamental assumptions or logic that sustains reality into question. And this, exactly, is where anguish emerges. The paradox that subverts the logic of inside-outside subverts the imaginary outlines of the body, those that separate between individual and surroundings. In the absence of such a distinction, the person experiences a regressive fusion in which her separate existence is under threat. This is a logical-topological-spatial form of the threat of incestuous engulfment which undoes the differences between inside and outside and actually undoes individuation. For Lacan, thus, there is, at the very root of anguish a terror of engulfment (rather than for instance of abandonment). This insight, obviously, has many clinical implications. When a child suffers from anxieties, and parents, in response, keep him close to themselves, this may actually exacerbate his anxieties as the child actually needs separateness. Logic is grounded in negation, yielding the taboo on incest which is the foundation of the structure of the family. Where logic is overturned this is tantamount to breaking the taboo.

Because, according to Lacan, it is the only affect that does not deceive anguish is extremely valuable from the clinical perspective (Harari, 2001, pp. 42 & 44). Since the libidinal investment of objects always involves the constitution of a phantasmatic myth that situates or construes the object (and desire), objects are always deceptive. Money as an object of desire implies a wish for respect, attractiveness, establishing one's image, etc. It is an endless metonymic chain: behind each seemingly ultimate object lurks another even more perfect object, and so on. Anguish however does not deceive because it has no object, because it exposes the appearance of "objectality". Hence the clinical encounter with anguish offers a kind of compass in the earlier mentioned process of crossing the phantasm (to which I will return at length in the final chapter). Anguish assists in identifying the jouissance which the patient won't give up or, differently put: in pinpointing the lack she does not accept—in the sense that she identifies herself as filling the lack, as the other's object of desire or jouissance. Though the filling of this lack produces jouissance, it is a jouissance that ensnares the subject, turning it into an object while not enabling it to take its place as a desiring subject.

Anguish is structurally inherent to psychoanalysis since it manifests itself in any patient facing the earlier mentioned fundamental analytical position: "I don't want anything from the patient." When the patient does not know what the analyst wants of her she feels anguish (Lacan, 1962, session 1). Or more precisely: it is in the face of the other's desire when that desire is mysterious to us, that we experience anguish. In the already mentioned story of Isaac's binding, Lacan argues that it isn't in regard to the horror of the binding that anguish arises but due to the uncertainty concerning God's will (Lacan, 2013). When the analyst wants nothing from the patient the latter will have to invent the demands and desires of the analyst in order to get rid of the anguish: the analyst wants my money, the analyst wants me to heal, the analyst wants me to bring in dreams for interpretation, and so on. This transference-generated projection of wishes reveals the phantasmatic structures that underlie the symptoms by means of which the patient exists as a wanted and wanting individual. Neurotic patients are on the one hand marked by their powerful resistance to situating themselves as an other's object of jouissance since taking such a position—by the logic of neurosis— involves obviating the lack, hence threatening the subject, and this triggers their anguish (Harari, 2001, p. 45). The fantasy, on the other hand, whereby something is demanded of them enables them to sacrifice a degree of jouissance while also maintaining themselves as subject—like the lizard who leaves its tail in the attacker's maw. Demand also clashes with symbiotic harmony and absolves them from anguish (makes them lacking),[1] but this neurotic dynamic comes at the price of repressing their own desires for the benefit of the other's wishes. Anguish therefore emerges between their positioning as the object of the other's desire (the threat of being turned into an object) and their longing in so far as they are subjects (original anguish, as Freud defined it, in the face of repressed drives).

Depression and suicide

Depression can occur in any of the four clinical structures. In the neurotic structure depression can be a side effect of a certain tactic that construes the subject's desire. So obsessive persons will position themselves as victims of an Imaginary Other. While this invention of the Other allows them to yearn by assuming that something is being required of them (just like the fitness trainer, by appointing her to be demanding with me it I achieve what I want)—this invented Other may at times become counterproductive, turning judgmental and oppressive. To free themselves from their depression, obsessive patients must come to see how they imagine themselves captive to the authority figure. They must, more specifically, learn to identify what desire this structure sustains— for instance blaming themselves rather than admitting that they are powerless.

While obsessive people are depressed by their sense of guilt, hysterical people are depressed because they feel inferior. Because frustration (distress, envy of others who have what they lack), for them, functions as the very core of longing, hysterical patients are constantly frustrated.

Where this frustration becomes excessive, here too, hysterical people will have to learn to pinpoint the drama they invent for the purpose of sustaining their desire.

People with perversities ground their existence in jouissance and when this becomes impossible for some reason (because the object of pleasure is forbidden or the fetish is no longer libidinally invested), they sink into a depression. That is when they may seek treatment. As for psychotic people, due to their difficulty in attaching themselves to the Symbolic system they will require external symbolic institutions in order to exist as subjects. When they find themselves outside the symbolic fabric for some reason (having lost their jobs or due to divorce) they are likely to become depressed much more than the neurotic subject. Because psychotic people's delusions provide them with a mission by way of replacing the symbolic function, when they shed these delusions they are bound to feel a lack of purpose and reason. Inventing a reason for living (Lacan calls this *sinthome* and he illustrates it by reference to James Joyce's self-fashioning as a writer as a *sinthomatic* solution) may have the effect of "stitching" psychotic people back into life and releasing them from the grip of depression.

Suicidal behaviour, too, like any other symptom, includes a core of the Real which is immune to interpretation. In the suicidal symptom, this core of the Real, of the drives, may be more powerful than in other types of symptom, so that understanding the source of the wish to die or the meaning articulated by this wish may not necessarily suffice for patients to give up on their destructive impulses. In such cases, speech as such may take the sting out of the death drive. If speech takes patients from the domain of the Real to that of the Symbolic (Lacan, 1961, session 13), then the more they put their pull toward death into words, the grip of the Real will weaken. This is why analysts' concern about discussing suicidality (as though it may encourage suicide) is unwarranted; talk about the death drive links subjects into life. It is the Real as death drive that tempts the suicidal person into silence and homeostasis. It is the symbolic linguistic realm that holds the subject in the only life available to her, human life. That is the logic behind talking about death wishes that makes them less powerful.

There are other cases when suicidal wishes or acts may be considered attempts to communicate something about desire: to be able to choose their desire, patients may have raised death as the alternative. Due to the tyranny of norms or of humiliating super-ego figures, patients may push aside their desires. They may refuse to acknowledge them for the sake of social acceptability. But when the alternative is death, then they will be able to go with their desires. The suicidal symptom posits death as the alternative in order then to choose desire. Suicidality, in other words, may either be subjects' attempt to bring upon themselves life-endangering conditions that will allow them to choose for their desire, or alternatively it may constitute an attempt to kill a humiliating, tyrannical figure with whom (or with whose injunctions) they identify. And it is in fact a good thing to disempower the figure of the tyrant. Where the need is pressing and life is in danger, the analyst may want to pinpoint the figure who more than anyone else is identified with the torturing super-ego so as to humiliate and squash it in order to remove the patient from under its crushing boot.

CHAPTER SIX

Clinical structures as subject positions

Viewing the human being as a subject, Lacanian ethics does not think of the symptom as pointing at something out there in objective reality in the same way that, say, a cough points in the direction of a flu. It considers the symptom as a mechanism that construes reality, in the manner of a traffic sign creating a reality whereby a certain street does not allow cars to enter. Lacanian clinical diagnostics, therefore, does not rely on symptoms as objective indicators but turns to the text of the patient as a reflection of styles of reality construction. The way in which patients use language—indeed, how they position themselves in it—reveals the different modes in which desire is construed in the clinical diagnostic structures. In other words, the various ways in which patients use language to sustain desire, the ways in which their very body is linked into language—are either neurotic (whether hysterical or obsessive), perverse, or psychotic modes (Skriabine, 2004).

A patient who complains that he checks obsessively whether the door is closed will be diagnosed—in positivist, medical, and descriptive manner—as obsessive. Because the Lacanian approach generates diagnosis in the course of speech—and if the patient presents the symptom through a statement that conveys "Let's see how you manage to get me to drop this symptom"; that is, if he structures the analyst as master and himself as the one who questions the master's mastery—then there may be good reason to diagnose as hysterical structure. In any case, the diagnosis serves as a working hypothesis that helps clinicians position themselves with regard to their patients. It is likely not to be useful or even outright damaging to approach neurotic persons as though they were psychotic or the other way around. Thus, for instance an interpretation referring to ambiguity in the patient's words may be harmful if he is psychotic and trying desperately to hold on to one reality, while insisting on one reality—in the face of having to make up his mind between various possibilities—in the work with a neurotic patient will rob him of the opportunity to emerge as a subject.

The central concepts of the Freudian-Lacanian clinical structures are the subject, the Other (capitalised to differentiate from the other), and the object—and their interrelations are what produces the clinical patterns of desire. Hence, when diagnosis refers to a structure, it is the structure of relations between subject, object, and the Other. In the hysterical structure the subject positions her or himself as the missing object of the Other, in myths and phantasms which all share the logic of: "Let's see you catching me, you never will." Hysterical individuals seduce but don't surrender. They exist by way of lack, something that was left out of the system: for instance, a person will come late in order to be noticed. In doing so she will either create or support the other's desire; she will find fault with the other, aiming to expose the other's lack yet at the same time she will refuse being satisfied: in other words, she also preserves her own lack.

In the obsessive structure the individual assumes the position of the Other who will not give up the object. This person, in other words, is subject to the injunction to make up for the lack, to hold on to the object so it won't escape him or else he might be missing the lost, nostalgic object which he is intent to complete himself with it. It is this command that fuels his desire. It is equally likely for the obsessive person to take the position of the object who needs to complete the Other (Lacan, 1961, session 22).

Both hysterical and obsessive people, by way of preserving their subject position, refuse to take the place of the other's object of jouissance. But while hysterical people wish to be the object of desire, obsessive people will feel wretched in this position. They fear being tempted to gratify the other: after all the object of their jouissance is the other's demand. This is manifest in obsessive people's tendency to take projects and tasks upon themselves (tasks that come to appear like a demand they must meet).

The perverse structure involves taking the object position in the face of an Other whom the person simultaneously does and does not complete.[1] The Other, in the perverse structure, does not long or demand as he or she does in neurosis: the Other's lack is in doubt. The Other assumes the form of the function of the Father, who is simultaneously present (as is the case with neurotic persons) and absent (as with psychotic persons). Often, as the Father embodies the Law, perverse people challenge the law. Wishing to expose its insufficiency, they taunt the law to make itself manifest—and they do this for instance by means of being delinquent, seemingly testifying to the absence of the Father-Law (Lacan, 1988 [1953], p. 221). Perverse people's objectal attitude blocks their ability to have fantasies and hence also their capacity for sexual activity between subjects, which relies on the existence of a fantasy that creates a gap between them. After all, fantasy is about what is lacking. Whether masochists or fetishists (who identify with objects, i.e., things), perverse individuals find jouissance in the object. Neurotic have perverse fantasies; pervert subjects have acts. Even the sadists who consider themselves the tools of natural forces or of gods, the object of the Other—Moloch, for instance, on whose behalf they make their sacrifice.

The psychotic structure applies to the position of an object that has not separated from the Other. Here structure as such comes into question as structure requires reciprocity between its parts. Paranoia—typical of the psychotic structure—instantiates the enduring presence of the Other from whom the psychotic person is not separate. Psychotic people don't manage to remove themselves from the position of being the object of jouissance of the other. This is most evident in the case of erotomania where individuals believe they are uncommonly attractive, due to which they are unstoppably persecuted by the jouissance of the other (since they are not separate from the other). Similarly, psychotic people experience their own drives as an attack against themselves, coming from the outside (Lacan, 1992 [1955], pp. 42–43).

The logic of clinical structures

The paradigm of the structure I describe now is the oedipal configuration, in which the mother is the place of the Other, the child in that of the object, and the father serves as the function that separates mother from child as part of the so-called oedipal complex. For Freud, the clinical structures were like so many points on the oedipal continuum; Lacan translated these terms into a logical language of elements in a structure. This logical language affords different metaphors: in one of these the mother can be identified as the Other, and the child as the object, in another the body is the Other and body parts are the object.

Its initial positioning as the mother's object (her phallus, as I will explain below), as what fills up her lack, is vital to the infant's survival. If an infant is superfluous from birth, there is no reason for its existence. Subjects may, in extreme circumstances, compensate for this by means of a delusion, which is fundamentally an invented destiny, a myth that justifies their existence in the world (the role of the messiah who serves God is a common delusion). A child who is born to meet a need (lack) in the mother will have to separate from her in order to exist as a subject. As said, the paternal function is to effect this separation of the child who constitutes a source of jouissance for her (in the psychotic structure, as mentioned before, the subject fails to move away from being an object of jouissance, which exposes him to grandiose, paranoid, and erotomanic delusions). Being symbolic, the paternal function does not require an actual father. "You have to get an injection because that's what the doctor said", or "The policeman does not allow me to use the car if I don't put this belt around you" are illustrations of how the name of the father is installed.

Another facet of separation occurs where the child finds itself competing: there are things the mother desires and that give her pleasure other than the child (the father, her career, another baby). The child, one might put it, stops serving as the (total) solution to her lack, as her phallus (the subject takes the position of the phallus in the psychotic structure; in the perverse structure that of an existing/non-existing—phallus). A transition occurs from a logic of yes or no being a phallus; to be either a supplementary object, a thrown away object, or not to be at, to identifying with the father as having a phallus, or, to taking the position of a subject with a lack and a desire.

In Lacanian logic, phallisation is a function of symbolisation. The penis serves as a paradigm for an organ that may and may not exist (the child learns that in the case of women it doesn't exist, and this teaches the child about the possibility of lack, absence). Its naming, or in other words: its isolation as an organ from the rest of the body, sustains its existence. More accurately: it is the very possibility of existence versus non-existence that marks something as having existence, i.e., gives it the phallic status of a distinct and meaningful object. The paradigm of the phallic function is, clearly, the distinction between the sexes—but in Lacanian thinking it refers to any kind of function of naming and differentiation.

It follows that reality is symbolic and that things are sustained by definitions. Lacan illustrates this by means of Aristotle's definition of mammals (Lacan, 1961, session 12): If we distinguish mammals from other animals by means of the presence of one singular sign, the "nipple", then the nipple must exist as something that can be seen separately from the rest of the body (only this will enable us to say that there are animals with and without nipple). Hence reality is symbolic: it emerges through a loss of the Real. The actual nipple must be lacking (among the non-mammals) for it to attain the status of a singular sign, which can then point at existence. Or, in other words: the signifier isolates something of the actual inchoate world, which then exists as a kind of presence-absence. This is why Lacan adopted Hegel's observation that the word kills the thing, but not without adding that this is the condition for the thing's rebirth by way of a concept. Subjectivity is enfolded in this dialectic of presence-absence (the phallus). The formation of the signifier based on the missing object, i.e., on the phallic dialectic between presence and absence, is a saliently logical moment in the rise of the subject. From now on, humans can no longer escape their tragic fate of being situated in language: subject to the law and to lack, and destined to live their desire.

In Lacanian logic, the function of the father in the oedipal triangle— the function of the law in the social context—not only regulates jouissance but also, paradoxically, generates desire. The organic instincts which the law governs are not identical to the urges and desires typical to subjects. The latter are the outcome of the modification they undergo through the function of the father, or in more abstract terms: through the substitution of the thing by the signifier. The clinical structures can be understood as tactics of desire and modes of being in the face of this paradoxical state of affairs.

Two positions can be observed in the neurotic structure: identification with the phallus, which brings along an anxiety of losing it (this is the fear of castration typical of the obsessive position), and identification with the absent phallus and the subsequent position of demanding one (the penis envy characteristic of the hysterical position). We can say that the obsessive person maintains desire by treating lack as a threat which must be denied, whereas the hysterical person does the same by means of treating lack as an unfair situation about which she or he complains.

Since the law of the father protects obsessive people from the jouissance of the mother, they stay very close to the law. Rather than helping them to desire, however, the law of the father leads them to fall back on procedure from a wish to do "the right thing"—at the expense of dealing with the question of their desire. Such people experience guilt facing the demandingness of the other they have constituted and the impulses of their jouissance. They sustain the figure of the father by means of guilt (the underlying logic is: "If I am guilty, then I am not fatherless, and hence I am protected against jouissance") in a way that preserves the denial of lack by means of the Other of causality, without whom they would encounter the anxiety of arbitrariness and indifference. Guilt compensates for the pain and distress of the encounter with the arbitrary, offering obsessive people meaning and hope along these lines: "If it's my responsibility and mistake then I can change it and prevent it."

Perceiving the other as demanding, the obsessive person withdraws to the intra-subjective domain, into his own thoughts. From a belief that once he was whole (possessed the phallus) he now tries to protect his perfection against constant erosion by means of a fantasy of a nostalgic lost paradise from before the arrival of the castrating father. He also finds it hard to tolerate lack in the other so he attempts to fill it. As he avoids lack, and hence his own desire, his own existence is not obvious to him, and thoughts become a way of certifying his existence. Obsessive doubt is the effect of refusing to rely on the Symbolic (signifiers) pretension about sustaining reality, and thought is an attempt to prove the existence of the actual by symbolic means. This is obviously a paradoxical effort and it is doomed to fail. It leads to obsessive thinking, like for instance "How do I know that I know?" (which is fundamentally the unconscious question: "How do I know that I exist?").

Hysterical individuals, by contrast, inhabit the inter-subjective domain between themselves and the other. In need of the other so he or she can frustrate them (thus feeding their own lack) they also take the role of frustrating the other—for this is their way of sustaining the other. Since their own form depends on pinpointing lack in the other, and since their existence becomes meaningful by seeing themselves as somehow diminished by the other, they must always place

lack in the other. Hysterical persons, moreover, tend to take an antag-
onistic stance *vis-a-vis* representations of the law, which possess the
phallus they lack. They would like to reveal the truth, namely that the
lawgiver, too, is castrated. And after all, that's how it is: there are some
laws above which humans cannot put themselves (the law of the jungle,
for instance, or death). Nevertheless, hysterical people, in order to hold
on to their desire, will persistently protest against the imputed potency
of the law and simultaneously in response to their own tendency to
both deny what is absent from the law and idealise the other (something that obstructs their desire—which is why they uncover the lack of
the other, and so on).

Hysterical people's main mode of representing lack (the gap between
language and actual existence, which does not yield to conceptualisation, and on whose account the individual transforms into a desiring subject) is by means of the metaphor of sexual difference. If lack
defines the subject, then lack of the phallus in sexual difference defines
the female position. Whether anatomically male or female, hysterical
people are frustrated by the lack they constitute as representations of
the absent phallus. When a patient says: "I don't have ..." the question
is whether this is his way to situate himself on the female side of sexual
difference and to respond to the question: "What is woman?"—"The
one who has not" (Lacan, 1992 [1955], p. 170).

Unlike obsessive people who blame themselves, hysterical people
refer to the law, mostly in order to blame others. Given their experience
of unjust deprivation, they can only hope for a better future—one in
which their complaint is heard and met. Such a future, needless to say,
never comes. Not only because humans are doomed to experience lack.
In addition, they also defer their own gratification (they preserve, that is,
their lack) so as to sustain desire, their subjectivity. Hysteria may sometimes be marked by individuals' resistance to recognise their responsibility both in the freedom to choose as well as for their fate, something
that is necessary to promote transference and the analysis (in such cases,
obviously, the question concerning the patients' responsibility for their
fate must be asked gently, having considered their readiness to confront
their responsibility without feeling blamed (Fink, 1997, p. 161)).

The classic partnership between a hysterical wife and an obsessive husband is not only a source of suffering but can also yield moments of comic
relief: The more effort the obsessive husband makes to satisfy his wife,
the more intense her refusal to be satisfied. The degree to which they are

able to recognise that the discrepancy, here, is structural will determine whether the narrative of their relationship evolves as tragedy or comedy. In comedy we accept the lack in the beginning, in tragedy at the end.

Unlike neurotic people, people with perversions do not have the ability to enjoy longing as such, i.e., fantasy. For such individuals, an unrealised fantasy means sheer suffering so they must act to find pleasure in the world. Perverse urges are not exclusive to perverse individuals. They are an integral part of sexuality. The ability to fantasise is part of the space the father opens between child and mother as he installs the phallic function that separates them. But in the case of the perverse structure this space opens only some of the way. Only half believing in the phallic function of the father, the perverse person does not have a stable relation with the father figure. The paradigmatic father figure, for the perverse person, is the father who, in the outside world, is perceived as very respectable, and who, at home, is humiliated by the mother. It could be that the father places himself at a masochistic, humiliated position but since in many cases it is the mother who introduces the father to the child, there is a limit to his control of the situation. The common association between perversion and social deviance results from the fact that perverse people dedicate themselves to sustaining the father as law exactly by means of challenging the law and diverging from it. As he was torturing his victims, the Marquise de Sade would address God: "That we see in Sade at every moment mingled, woven together with one another, invective—I mean invective against the Supreme Being, his negation being only a form of invective even if it is the most authentic negation" (Lacan, 1961, p. 185). Perverse individuals keep offending against the law in order to maintain it through its failure, while simultaneously deriving pleasure from the implications of their offense, namely: non-separation from the object, i.e., the mother.

The position typical of perversion is associated with taking an objectal place, as a phallus which is and is not a distinct part of the mother's body (an additional expression of the existence and non-existence of the separating phallic function in the perverse structure).Thus perverse persons take pleasure in turning themselves into the other's object of jouissance, in removing themselves from the temporal dimension, thereby annihilating themselves by way of desiring subjects (but they don't experience the other's pleasure in them as persecutory as would be the case in psychosis). This is why perverse individuals take pleasure in objects that are like prostheses of the mother's body, such as a shoe or an item of underwear, which must be both close to their body and yet distinct from it, so that identification with them yields the pleasure of non-total separation from the mother. Masochist pleasure, too, fundamentally inheres in the subject's positioning as a rejected object (contrary to common assumptions, pleasure, here, does not derive from pain as such). Since the function of the father is absent, it is derived from the mother by means of her identification with the rejected object. The position of the one who is humiliated encapsulates the perverse duality of being part of the mother's body while being rejected by it at one and the same time (Lacan, 1961, session 15). As for sexual difference, perverse people erase it by turning the representation of the phallic organ into their sexual partner (whether it is a thing, as in fetishism, or the human figure itself, as in voyeurism or necrophilia).

Perverse individuals, as a rule, don't turn to treatment as long as reality offers them access to their pleasure: only when the source of pleasure is no longer available or has become prohibited will they seek treatment. In these circumstances, no longer able to recover the loss by appealing to their fantasy, they are bound to become depressed.

In the case of the psychotic subject, the experience of, "Why can everyone make sense of it except for me?" is frequent. One patient, for instance, said that he could no longer bear the arbitrary nature of his employer's orders. He only felt comfortable with instructions whose logic he could follow. Rather than questioning the law, he suffered a sense of alienation regarding the function of the law, of the Other. Such a failure is more fundamental. It turns the law into something persecutory or unbearable. This is why psychotic people often long to feel guilty like other, normal people. Unlike neurotic people, who are exposed to repressed materials through their associations or dreams, psychotic subjects don't repress insufferable materials: they reject them. These materials, in their perspective, pop up from somewhere outside of them in the form of hallucinations and delusions. They experience these as real and alien. Because psychotic individuals do not experience the lack between subject and other as natural, they have difficulty developing emotionally intimate relations as the latter depend on the existence of a gap, a lack. Since infatuation involves an experience of lack, a type of longing for a person, even in their presence; or alternatively, the wish to be meaningful in filling the other's lack; states of infatuation—with their implication of lack in the other which the psychotic person is unable to fill—may trigger a psychotic crisis.

The analyst's position in transference relations as a function of the patient's structure

Since the function that creates meaning is intact in neurotic people, any event or word can have a plethora of meanings. Neurotic patients, therefore, are curious about unconscious meanings and assume the analyst knows something about them. The analyst becomes a figure of the unconscious for such patients (thus a patient may say that the analyst probably thinks that something means this or that, or dream that the analyst is talking to him—such things may be knowledge from the patient's unconscious).

Rather than being based on behavioural symptoms, the distinction between hysteria and obsession, as said, is determined under conditions of transference. Hysterical patients, in the interpersonal domain, will show curiosity about the analyst as a person—they will ask questions about the analyst's private life, be on the lookout for the analyst's failures, will protest against the formal conditions of the treatment, and will want to be the analyst's favourite and most interesting patient. They will put the analyst on a pedestal in order later to topple her or him. There's usually never a dull moment in the therapeutic work with hysterical patients.

While hysterical individuals formulate their lack in terms of sexual difference, obsessive persons put it in terms of life and death (Fink, 1997, p. 161), with death serving as the yardstick which imbues life with meaning. Construing an Other who commands that they resign their jouissance, obsessive individuals are captive to the myth that once the father dies, they will have access to full pleasure, free of guilt. But in reality, the dead father still serves to keep the obsessive person from his or her pleasure. Freud's Rat Man, for instance, went on suffering from guilt toward his father long after the latter's death. This is how obsessive people maintain themselves in a reality in which they stand accused. This is why in the transference they will ignore both the analyst's signs of life and their own signs of lack; this is why they will ascribe intentions and instructions to the analyst, and will find it hard to come up with free associations if the analyst does not prompt them. In the face of this kind of transference, analysts will assert their vitality—concretely, by coughing, moving, etc., or alternatively by leaving questions unanswered, in order to break through their obsessive patient's hermetic position.

Since in the case of psychosis repression doesn't play a prominent role, patients have no curiosity about the hidden meanings of their actions and behaviours, nor do they consider the analyst as an oracle who knows something about the unconscious. Transference will take the form of the attribution of medical-technical knowledge to the analyst. Living with a sense that everybody but them has access to reality and social relations, they regard the analyst as a representative of the social order who validates reality for them. In other instances, psychosis may be marked by absolute certainty, and any attempt by the analyst to question this certainty will be experienced as persecutory. Here it is analysts' role to provide the external structure that maintains the psychotic patient as a subject: to constitute a steady anchor in the patient's life, possibly for protracted stretches of time. Analysts must learn these patients' language thereby to join them. They may well be among the few people in patients' life who speak their tongue.

Perverse patients are not typically keen to find out about their unconscious or their own desire. This is because rather than longing for the object they usually take pleasure in it—or in being the object themselves. When their source of jouissance runs dry, they seek treatment. In the transference, the analyst will be reduced, much like most other people in the perverse person's life, to an object position.

CHAPTER SEVEN

The end of treatment

As Lacan saw it, on reaching its conclusion analysis produces an analyst. This is not necessarily the case for therapies that are not defined as psychoanalysis. The metaphors for the analytic process and for its (mostly logical) end point which Lacan proposed are useful in guiding treatment even if it isn't psychoanalysis.

Identification as object

As mentioned already, the neurotic patient refuses to be an object. But in declining to be the object of jouissance of some persona on the Imaginary plane (in order thus to avoid erasure of his subjecthood), he also makes it paradoxically difficult for himself to desire, that is, to be a subject, on the Symbolic plane. Desire exists only as part of the structure of the Symbolic chain, of the ideas and concepts that make up the social structure as it changes from one generation to the next. At the end of the analysis, therefore, the person will ideally identify as object of the Symbolic order. At this juncture, subject and object, desire and jouissance, will have become one.

To put it differently, though it may transpire at the end of the treatment that the Imaginary other does not really exist, this should not entail that he is superfluous, that he cannot be put to use. One may use a compass even if one does not intend to reach the furthest reaches of the North Pole, much like there's no need for a scientific proof of the existence of God in order to pray to him. While the big Other is demanding and judgmental at the onset of the analysis, at its end he may be employed to set boundaries to jouissance and the production of desire. If, at the start of the analysis, the neurotic patient may pay his personal fitness trainer in order for him to make him work hard, feel that he is tormenting him and that he is working for the trainer, at the end of it he will understand that he pays him for his own good.

The psychoanalytic clinic is constructed in such a way that the psychoanalyst serves as a component supporting the structure of the patient's subjecthood. Thus, the analytic position involves positioning oneself as object (which is why a certain alleviation of neurosis is required in order to achieve taking one's position as an analyst). The analyst, whose main wish is to offer treatment, takes position as object of the patient's thoughts and desires. By maintaining silence, he pushes the patient to speak; by occupying the position of object (who exits the patient's life at the end of the treatment) he drives the patient into subject position.[1]

Lacan also points out that the identification as object of the symbolic structure opens up the possibility for a link with the eternal. He makes the distinction between the first death—the moment when word kills thing (concept substitutes for the Real) and the second death, namely biological death. As identification with the signifier is possible, and the latter of course remains unaffected by biological death, Lacan argues that the signifier generated by the first death survives the second death. Symbolic immortalisation survives biological death. This formulation by Lacan is a logical rendering of Freud's myth of *Totem and Taboo*. Freud described the totemic system as a solution to the males' turn against the alpha male, which would leave the tribe without a real leader. The role of the primordial father was attributed to a mythical-imaginary animal which could not be killed. An immortal symbol of leadership solved the problem of the leader's actual death.

Usually the symbol that survives biological death is a memorial, a tomb, a person's name, his symbolic function or some creation he left behind. This is neither religious faith nor mysticism: the fact is that symbols survive humans, and that identification with symbols, with the Symbolic system, extends existence beyond temporal linearity (Lacan,

1961, session 26). Lacan referred to Antigone as one who acknowledged she had no existence as subject outside the structure of the order of the family. This explains her willingness to die in order to bury her brother and to survive second death.

Traversing the phantasm, discarding identifications, and identification with the symptom

The phantasm is a particular type of fantasy. It is a myth of perfection which serves as a tool of jouissance. Symptoms are not directly related to the existence of the phantasm but to belief in it, to a failure of recognition of the fact that phantasm misleads. When he believes in phantasmatic perfection, the subject will need symptoms to undermine that perfection because the latter erases him as subject. Recognition of the fact that the phantasm is a myth, which is achieved through a process Lacan calls "traversing the phantasm", involves recognition that lack cannot be eliminated (and that myth only comes to support jouissance). Lacan, in order to represent acceptance of lack, borrows Freud's notion of "castration". Thus, for a masochist traversing the phantasm will take the form of recognition of the fact that he structures reality so as to situate himself as a rejected object (or, in the case of hysteria, as being frustrated; or as a perfectionist in the case of obsession) with the aim to hold on to his faith in perfection. Traversing the phantasm renders the suffering of the symptom superfluous and allows the subject to use the symptom as a tool of desire. The symptom is a complaint only in comparison to the wholeness of the phantasm. For Lacan, this process of accepting lack is a movement away from impotence (the thought that the lack could have been dealt with if it were not for the subject's failure) to impossibility (the realisation that lack is inevitable part of existence). This shift results in a great sense of relief. Once one recognises the Symbolic-Imaginary, virtual nature of reality, as desire constructs it, the difference between this invented, ideal reality, with all its associated identifications, and the Real—which is impenetrable to change—becomes patent.

Fantasy allows for identification. For people with neuroses, too, the fantasy is a kind of delusion which gives the subject a function, allowing him to define and identify himself. Some therapeutic approaches consider this identification an important objective, and patients often start their treatment by asking the analyst to tell them who they are. At the end of the process of analytical psychotherapy, the patient is no longer interested in self-definition: the attempt to reduce being so as to fit a definition also involves reducing desire. But desire is metonymic in nature and doesn't fix on one image of identification. Considering identification as an object of a structure implies the continuous motion of desires which are never fixed in a stable unitary identity. If the Imaginary register enables the consolidation of a fictive identity, thus releasing the person from the chaos of the Real, though at the price of a congealed, frozen ego, free association helps the subject to position himself among signifiers in a way that gives him freedom of movement and disburdens him of the stagnation of imaginary self-definition.

This process, which Lacan calls "crossing of the plane of identification", involves the recognition that desire exists in us and that it, rather than our idealised self-perception, is what determines us (Lacan, 1978 [1963], p. 273). Still, unlike Buddhists, Lacan concedes that despite the dangers of identification with it, the ego also is an important component of erotic jouissance. While in his early teaching, Lacan focused on the diverse modes of undoing the Imaginary ego, in his later work he stressed the need for the combined activity of the three orders (the Symbolic, the Imaginary, and the Real) (Lacan, 1975, session 10).

Lacan also refers to identification with desire at the end of analysis as identification with the symptom. Once the Symbolic and Imaginary dimensions of the symptom, i.e., whatever it conveys concerning the subject's desire, have been interpreted and the symptomatic suffering has been alleviated, the symptom nevertheless always retains a germ of Real, a germ of jouissance which no amount of interpretation can resolve. Then what's left to do is to stop treating this germ as a problem but to identify with it; what remains is to observe where our feet are taking us in order thus to understand where we want to go (Soler, 2003, pp. 250–252).

Have you acted in accordance with the desire that is in you?

At the conclusion of the seminar on the ethics of psychoanalysis, Lacan discusses life from the perspective of the following bottom-line question: "Have you acted in conformity with the desire that is in you?" (Lacan, 1992 [1959], p. 314). Desire: that is to say—not wish, of which the self is the agent, and which, therefore, flows from the ego. Rather, desire as master, imposing itself on the subject (in the sense of the one who is being subjected to it; and hence the question formulates: the *desire in you* not the *desire of you*), but also desire which the subject has the power to subserve. The subject is the subject of the structure of the unconscious. Desire is its effect and simultaneously it drives and maintains the subject. Desire is not the same as the wish for goods, for acquisition; it is, quite on the contrary, the thing for which one is ready to forego worldly goods and property, for which one is willing to pay (Lacan, 1992 [1959], pp. 310–323). Hence the question about the desire inside the subject is asked in the context of the Day of Judgment, the bottom line. Does the act I choose to commit now follow the same direction as what I would like to prevail after my death? Does the act I choose to commit now follow the same direction as what may be chosen by one looking back at his choices on his deathbed? These questions are, of course, posed under a certain constraint. To what extent can we know what we, as future subjects on our deathbed, will want?

Though pharmacology and cognitive approaches today play the prime role in the amelioration of psychic suffering in the western world, psychoanalysis, in its various guises and its diverse practices and institutions, still endures. Strikingly, it still relates the treatment of the symptom to a life of desire and meaning rather than to a religious imperative or other normativities. Humanity still benefits from the gift Freud offered when he discovered the unconscious. Still, words have a capacity to remove bodily pain as by an act of witchcraft, to spark desire where previously depression reigned, or to dispel anguish and replace it with yearning. Still, belief in something that exceeds us prevails: the unconscious which originates in us, for which we may humbly take responsibility without suffering guilt—humility that is a cure in and of itself. Still, there are those who ask: "Do you act according to the desire in you?" and who will listen patiently until the question evokes a "Yes".

NOTES

Introduction

1. I use a universalising, inclusive masculine to refer to both genders.
2. Is the subject or the unconscious created or is it revealed? In a structuralist perspective, the distinction between creation and revelation disappears. In this perspective, the analytic discourse structures the subject as the subject of the unconscious by assuming its existence. I will elaborate on this in the chapter dedicated to the graph of desire.
3. "Enjoyment" would be the closest translation of Lacan's term *jouissance* which however is generally preserved as is in English Lacanian texts.

Chapter One

1. In this book, I refer to "word" and "signifier" interchangeably.
2. The Other with a capital O, rather than referring to a specific other, points at a symbolic system.
3. Information available online at: https://en.wikipedia.org/wiki/Zippy_the_Pinhead

Chapter Five

1. Perverse people, unlike neurotic people, do not object to being the object of jouissance (masochists, for example, actively strive for this, and fetishists identify with the object of jouissance). Psychotic patients fail to remove themselves from being in the position of the other's object of jouissance and they compensate for this by means of either paranoia or erotomania.

Chapter Six

1. For Lacan phobia is located halfway between perversion and neurosis: There is the possibility of perverse fusion, but while the perverse person would delight in such fusion, in the case of the phobia it arouses horror. Phobia can also be considered as the point of intersection between obsessive and hysterical neurosis. Either way: when a patient seeks therapy for phobias it is unclear what structure will be revealed once the lack is pinpointed.

Chapter Seven

1. Lacan relates this objectal position to the other jouissance—to the female position in matters of sexuality, or to the mystical position.

REFERENCES

Boothby, R. (1991). *Death and Desire*. New York: Routledge.

Chouraqui-Sepel, C. (2005). Angst and its English translation. Available online at: www.champlacanienfrance.net/article.php3?id_article=241

Efrati, D., & Israely, Y. (2007). *Hafilosofia ve hapsichoanaliza shel Jacques Lacan*. Tel Aviv: Universita meshuderet/Ministry of Defense: (In Hebrew).

Fink, B. (1997). *A Clinical Introduction to Lacanian Psychoanalysis*, Cambridge MA: Harvard University Press.

Fink, B. (2007). *Fundamentals of Psychoanalytic Technique*. New York: Norton.

Freud, S. (1900a). *The Standard Edition, Vol 4. The Interpretation of Dreams*. London: Vintage.

Freud, S. (1909d). *The Standard Edition, Vol 10. Notes Upon a Case of Obsessional Neurosis*. London: Vintage.

Freud, S. (1912e). *The Standard Edition, Vol 12. Recommendations to the Physicians Practicing Psycho-Analysis*. London: Vintage.

Freud, S. (1913m). *The Standard Edition, Vol 12. On Psychoanalysis*. London: Vintage.

Freud, S. (1914g). *The Standard Edition, Vol 12. Remembering, Repeating and Working Through*. London: Vintage.

Freud, S. (1919h). *The Standard Edition, Vol 17. The Uncanny*. London: Vintage.

Freud, S. (1920g). *The Standard Edition, Vol 18. Beyond the Pleasure Principle*. London: Vintage.

Freud, S. (1921c). *The Standard Edition, Vol 18. Group Psychology and the Analysis of the Ego*. London: Vintage.

Freud, S. (1926d). *The Standard Edition, Vol 20. Inhibition, Symptom and Anxiety*. London: Vintage.

Freud, S. (1930a). *The Standard Edition, Vol 21. Civilization and it's Discontent*. London: Vintage.

Harari, R. (2001). *Lacan's Seminar on Anxiety*. New York: Other Press.

Julien, P. (1995). *Jacques Lacan's Return to Freud: The Real, the Symbolic and the Imaginary*. New York: New York University Press.

Lacan, J. (2002 [1953]). *The Function and Field of Speech and Language in Psychoanalysis*. In: *Ecrits*. New York: Norton.

Lacan, J. (1988 [1953]). *The Seminar of Jacques Lacan, Seminar 1—Freud's Papers on Technique*. New York: Norton.

Lacan, J. (1988 [1954]). *The Seminars of Jacques Lacan, Book II—The Ego in Freud's Theory and in the Technique of Psychoanalysis*. New York: Norton.

Lacan, J. (1992 [1955]). *The Seminar of Jacques Lacan, Book III—The Psychoses*, New York: Norton.

Lacan, J. (2002 [1957]). *The Agency of the Letter in the Unconscious or Reason since Freud*. In: *Ecrits*. New York: Norton.

Lacan, J. (2002 [1958a]). *The Direction of the Treatment and the Principles of its Power*. In: *Ecrits*. New York: Norton.

Lacan, J. (2002 [1958b]). *The Mirror Stage as Formative of the Function of the I as Revealed in Psychoanalytic Experience*. In: *Ecrits*. New York: Norton.

Lacan, J. (1992 [1959]). *The Seminar of Jacques Lacan, Book VII—The Ethics of Psychoanalysis*. New York: Norton.

Lacan, J. (1960). Seminar VIII—Transference. Unpublished manuscript translated by Cormac Gallagher, Session 6.

Lacan, J. (2002 [1960]). *The Subversion of the Subject and the Dialectic of Desire in the Freudian Unconscious*. In: *Ecrits*. New York: Norton.

Lacan, J. (1961). Seminar IX—Identification. Unpublished manuscript translated by Cormac Gallagher, Session 1.

Lacan, J. (1962). Seminar X—Anxiety. Unpublished manuscript translated by Cormac Gallagher, Session 14.

Lacan, J. (1978 [1963]). *The Seminar of Jacques Lacan Book XI—The Four Fundamental Concepts of Psychoanalysis*. New York: Norton.

Lacan, J. (2002 [1964a]). Position of the Unconscious. In: *Ecrits*. New York: Norton.

Lacan, J. (2002 [1964b]). *On Freud's 'Trieb' and the Psychoanalyst's Desire*. In: *Ecrits*. New York: Norton.

Lacan, J. (1966). Seminar XIV—Logic of Phantasm. Unpublished manuscript translated by Cormac Gallagher, Session 5.

Lacan, J. (1974). Seminar XXII—RSI. Unpublished manuscript translated by Cormac Gallagher, Session 1.

Lacan, J. (1985). Intervention on Transference. In: R. Mitchell & J. Rose. *Feminine Sexuality*. New York: Norton.

Lacan, J. (2013). *On the Names of the Father*. Cambridge, UK: Polity Press.

Levi-Strauss, C. (1962). *Totemism*. Boston: Beacon.

Skriabine, P. (2004). *Clinic and Topology: The Flaw in the Universe*. In: E. Ragland, & D. Milovanovich. (Eds.), *Lacan: Topologically Speaking*. New York: Other Press.

Soler, C. (2003). *What Lacan Said About Women*. New York: Other Press.

Žižek, S. (2002). *Welcome to the Desert of the Real: Five Essays on September 11 and Related Dates*. London and New York: Verso.

INDEX

ambiguity
    and anti-fascist reality, 8
    belief in ego's unity to emergence
        of subject, 35
    and subject position, 7–9
"analysis", xiii
analyst
    desire of, 22–25
    position without reference
        to patient, 25–28
"analyst", xiii
    desire, 22–25
    without reference to patient,
        25–28
    training, xiv
    in transference relations, 84–85
analytic
    listening, 35–38
    space, 29
anguish, xv, 61, 69–72 *see also*:
        depression; trauma
    children development and sexual
        energy, 69

vs. depression, 69
"devil's elixirs, The", 70
objects, 71
and phantasm, 63–65
repression, 70
transference-generated projection
        of wishes, 72
anti-essentialism, 1–4 *see also*:
        desire-based reality
anti-fascist reality, 8
anxiety as repressed desire, xv

biographical and structural
        interpretation, 39–40
blame, 21
Boothby, R., 68

capitonnage, 8
cathartic effects, 20
Chouraqui-Sepel, C., 69
Claude Levi-Strauss' structuralist
        theory, 59
clinical structures, xviii

analyst's position in transference
        relations, 84–85
delusion, 78
dialectic of presence-absence, 79
Freudian-Lacanian clinical
        structures, 76
hysteria vs. obsession, 84
hysterical individuals, 76, 80–82
infatuation, 83
Lacanian clinical diagnostics, 75
law of the father, 80
logic of clinical structures, 77–83
neurotic patients, 77, 84
obsessive doubt, 80
obsessive people, 76, 81
oedipal complex, 78
oedipal configuration, 77
Other, The, 77
paranoia, 77
paternal function, 78
people with perversions, 82
perversion, 77, 85
phallisation, 78
positions in neurotic structure, 79
psychotic individuals, 83
reality, 79
subject, object, and the Other, 76
as subject positions, 75
transference, 85
clinic as symbolic space, 29 see also:
        interpretation
analytic listening and encouraging
        speech and desire, 35–38
biographical and structural
        interpretation, 39–40
cancellations and late arrivals,
        31–32
cutting session as act of
        interpretation, 45–47
desire, 36
dream interpretation, 42–44
ego and imaginary identification
        in early stages of treatment,
        34–35
first sessions, 33–34
interpretation, 38, 40–42

jouissance, 36
making notes, 32–33
mirror stage, 35
moving to couch as act of
        interpretation, 44–45
payment, 30–31
telephone conversation, 30
contemporary super-ego, 16
creation and revelation, 92
cultural environment formation, xiv
cutting sessions, xvi, 8

defense in transference, 49
delusions, 4, 78
demanding Other, the, 27
depression, xv, 3, 69
as lack of desire, xv
obsessive people, 72
people with perversities, 73
and suicide, 72–74
Descartes, 3
desire, 3, 12, 36, 87
acting in accordance with, 90–91
anguish as expression of
        repressed, xiv
anxiety as repressed, xv
depression as lack of, xv
ethics of, 18
as expression of repressed
        desire, xiv
identification as object, 87–89
identification with symptom, 89–90
loss of object as condition for, 9–10
pathology, xv
by symptom, xiv
unconscious, 7
desire-based reality, 1 see also: ethical
        foundations
ambiguity and anti-fascist reality, 8
ambiguity and subject position, 7–9
cutting session, 8
delusions, 4
depression, 3
experience of the Real, 10
imaginary castration, 13
imaginary register, 11

interpretation of meaning, 8
loss of the object as condition for
        desire, 9–10
miss-identification, 11
neurotic individuals, 5
Other, The, 12
perverse individuals, 6
psychotic people, 5
reality-generating mechanism, 6
registers of the real, imaginary,
        and symbolic, 10–13
Symbolic castration, 13
Symbolic Other, The, 12–13
Symbolic register, 11
unconscious desire, 7
validity of reality, 4–7
"devil's elixirs, The", 70
dialectic of truth, 53–54 *see also*:
        transference
dream, 42
interpretation, 42–44

Efrati, D., 2
ego and imaginary identification
        in treatment, 34–35
ethical foundations, 1 *see also*: desire-
        based reality; ethics
ethics, xiv, 13–18 *see also*: ethical
        foundations
analyst's desire, 22–25
analyst's position without reference
        to patient, 25–28
blame, 21
cathartic effects, 20
contemporary super-ego, 16
of desire, 18
dichotomy between inside
        and outside, 16
and esthetics, 18–19
of happiness, 14
jouissance, 14, 16
Kantian ethics, 15
of Lacanian psychoanalysis, 14
maternal super-ego, 15
Moebius strip, 17
Sade's ethics, 16

shedding belief in fullness, 20–22
sublimation as creativity, 19–20
super-ego, 15
symbolic function, 19
the demanding Other, 27
therapists and position of
        authority, 28

fantasy, 89
vs. phantasm, 65
Fink, B., 38, 81
Freudian insights, xiii
Freudian-Lacanian clinical
        structures, 76
Freudian slip, 6
Freudian unconscious, 2
Freud, S., 13, 36, 60
dream, 42
nirvana, 25
psychoanalysis, xiv
repetition compulsion, 2
roots of neurosis, 39
sublimation, 19
symptom, 60
three forms of identification, 50
transference, 49–50

guilt, 58

Harari, R., 71
Heraclitus, 1
hypochondria, 23
hysteria, 81
hysterical individuals, 76,
        80–81, 84
hysterical wife and obsessive
        husband, 81–82
vs. obsession, 81–82, 84

identification, 50–51
crossing of the plane of, 90
discarding, 89–90
forms of, 50
as object, 87–89
with symptom, 89–90
transference and, 50–51

identity as symbolic texture
        of words, xiv
Imaginary
    castration, 13
    at end of treatment, 87–88
    register, 11
    utopia, 23
infatuation, 83
inside and outside, 16
interpretation, 38 *see also*: clinic as
        symbolic space
    biographical and structural, 39–40
    confirmation for, 38
    cutting session as act of, 45–47
    dream, 42–44
    inhibitions and jouissance, 39
    of meaning, 8
    moving to couch as act of, 44–45
    object of, 41
    and truth, 40–42
Israely, Y., 2

jouissance, 14, 16, 36
    and defence, 55
    inhibitions and, 39
    paradoxical nature, 16
Julien, P., 27

Kant, 15
Kantian ethics, 15
Ka-Tzetnik, 68

Lacanian
    clinical diagnostics, 75
    ethics, xv
    notion of transference, 52–53
    psychoanalysis, 12, 14
    treatment, xiv
Lacan, J., xiii
    analysts' training, xiv
    anguish, xv
    assumption on reality, xiv
    attention to Freudian insights, xiii
    capitonnage, 8
    dichotomy between inside and
        outside, 16

Lacanian treatment, xiv
    patient's identity as symbolic
        texture of words, xiv
    reality is symbolical, xiv
    subjectivication, xiii
    symptom produces desire, xiv
    treatment's objectives and
        outcomes in ethical domain,
        xiv
    unconscious, 6
    view of reality as invention, 6
language, 11–12
law of the father, 80
Levi-Strauss, C., 59
    structuralist theory, 59

masochism, signs of, 65
maternal super-ego, 15
meaning, interpretation of, 8
metaphoric lack, 61
mirror stage, 35
miss-identification, 11
Moebius strip, 17

neurosis, 7
    roots of, 39
neurotic individuals, 5, 77, 84
neurotic misery, 13
neurotic patients, 77, 84
neurotics, 5
neurotic structure, 79
nirvana, 25

object, 9
objectal attitude, 77
obsession
    vs. hysteria, 84
    hysterical wife and obsessive
        husband, 81–82
    obsessive doubt, 80
    obsessive neurosis, 5
    obsessive people, 72, 76, 81
oedipal complex, 78
oedipal configuration, 77
Other, The, 12, 77, 92
    the demanding, 27

paranoia, 77
paternal function, 78
perversions, 82
    individuals', 6, 85, 93
    objectal attitude, 77
    people with, 6, 73, 82, 85, 93
    perverse structure, 77
    pleasure of non-total separation
        from mother, 83
    position typical of, 82
    structure, 77
phallisation, 78
phantasm, xviii, 89
    crossing the, 65
    fantasies vs., 65
    subject and object, 64
    symptom and, 63–65
phobia, 93
pleasure of non-total separation
        from mother, 83
pleasure principle, 3
presence-absence, dialectic of, 79
principle of conceptualization, 2
psychoanalysis
    Lacanian, xvi
    Symbolic register, 12
    using words to solve problems
        caused by words, xiv
psychoanalyst's starting position, xvii
psychoanalytic clinic, 88
psychoanalytic knowledge, xiii
psychosis, 85
    psychotic individuals, 83
    psychotic people, 5
    repression, 85

reality, xiv, 79
    assumption on, xiv
    ethical implication for, xv
    -generating mechanism, 6
    Lacan's basic assumption, xiv
    in philosophical premise, xv
    as symbolical, xiv
    validity of, 4–7
Real, the, 68
    experience of, 10

    and Symbolic, 62
register of the Real, 10
repetition, 2
    compulsion, 2
    escaping, 25
repressed desire
    anxiety as, xv
    expression of, xiv
repression
    anguish, 70
resistance and defence, 54–55

Sade, 15
Sade's ethics, 16
signifier, 2, 4
Skriabine, P., 75
Soler, C., 63, 90
story of Isaac's binding, 27
structuralist theory, 59
subject creation and revelation, 92
subjectivisation, xiii
sublimation, 19
    as creativity, 19–20
suicidal behaviour, 73–74
super-ego, 15
Symbolic castration, 13
symbolic function, 19
Symbolic Other, The, 12–13
Symbolic register, 11, 12
symbols, 88
symptom, 57
    anguish, 61
    assumption logic, 57
    as bastion of subject's singularity,
        58–63
    Claude Levi-Strauss' structuralist
        theory, 59
    conceptualisations of, 60
    as expression of repressed desire, xiv
    Freud, 60
    guilt, 58
    metaphoric lack, 61
    as outcome, 57–58
    and phantasm, 63–65
    produces desire, xiv
    Real and Symbolic, 62

therapists and position of authority, 28
transference, xvii, 49, 85
    dialectic of truth, 53–54
    element of defensiveness in, 49
    in Freudian sense, 49–50
    -generated projection of wishes, 72
    and identification, 50–51
    jouissance and defence, 55
    Lacanian notion of, 52–53
    resistance and defence, 54–55
    triggering, 52
trauma, 67–69
    collapse, 67
    Ka-Tzetnik, 68
    into memory, 68
    Real, the, 68
    therapeutic work with, 67
treatment, end of, xviii, 87
    acting in accordance with desire,
        90–91
    discarding identifications, 89–90
    fantasy, 89

identification as object, 87–89
identification with symptom, 89–90
imaginary, 87–88
phantasm, 89
psychoanalytic clinic, 88
symbols, 88
truth, dialectic of, 53–54

unconscious, 6
    creation and revelation, 92
    desire, 7

words
    patient's identity as symbolic
        texture of words, xiv
    precondition for the work with, xiv
    to solve problems caused
        by words, xiv

Yekhiel Dinur. *See* Ka-Tzetnik

Žižek, S., 68